DAVIS

RADICAL CHANGES,
DEEP CONSTANTS

5. 5. *Davis Enterprise* Printing Shop, c. 1925. *From the right: William H. Scott, Kathryn King Scott, an unidentified linotype operator, and the Reverend Nathan H. Fiske. Fiske was the moving spirit in Davis's "community Christianity" of the 1920s. (Larkey Collection.)*

Cover image: *On its cross-country tour, the 20 millionth Ford automobile stops at Liggett's Garage, 139 G Street, September 17, 1931.* *From the left in the first standing row are: an unidentified man; banker Frank Wray; Dollie Covell, mother of Mabel Liggett, who is next in line; Frank P. Liggett, owner of the garage; Chief of Police Floyd Gatrell; judge and* Enterprise *editor William Henry Scott; Frank P. Liggett Jr.; and, seated in the car, Mayor Calvin "Cal" Covell. (Hattie Weber Museum.)*

THE MAKING OF AMERICA

Davis

Radical Changes, Deep Constants

John Lofland

ARCADIA

Published by Arcadia Publishing,
Charleston SC, Chicago IL, Portsmouth NH, San Francisco CA

Printed in Great Britain.

Library of Congress Catalog Card Number: 2004102099

For all general information contact Arcadia Publishing at:
Telephone 843-853-2070
Fax 843-853-0044
E-Mail sales@arcadiapublishing.com
For customer service and orders:
Toll-Free 1-888-313-2665

Visit us on the Internet at http://www.arcadiapublishing.com

CONTENTS

ACKNOWLEDGMENTS

In writing this history of Davis, I have diligently used the work of four prior students of it: Joann Leach Larkey, Ann Scheuring, Mike Fitch, and William Diemer. I photocopied their publications and scissored them into bits that I sorted into the nine periods that organize this story. As numerous references to them attest, I have depended upon them to chart the way. Many thanks to Richard N. Schwab for transcribing George Pierce's daily journal and reviewing this book in draft.

In the later 1990s, I began visiting the Hattie Weber Museum of Davis most Wednesday afternoons and have chatted with Phyllis Haig, the curator. Frequently, I have had historical questions and she has had answers. Beyond specific information, I have greatly appreciated her treating me, a newcomer, as a fellow student of Davis history. Thanks, Phyllis.

Not wanting to write this book alone, I was happy to be able to recruit Dennis Dingemans to be the second author. Unfortunately, after some months he found he was not able to participate in the project and had to withdraw. When he left, I had gotten too far to stop, so I finished it. I therefore owe Dennis the unusual debt of causing me to decide to start. In addition, he is an expert on Davis history and has taught me much, for which I am very grateful.

Several people read all or almost all the book in draft and offered suggestions for revision that I have adopted and that have significantly improved it: Lynn Campbell (especially on periods 7 and 8); Laura Cole-Rowe (especially on the Downtown); Jon Li (especially on periods 8 and 9); and Ann Scheuring (especially on UC Davis). Frank Child, Blake Gumprecht, Gerald Heffernon, Katherine Hess, Virginia Issacs, Margaret Kautz, Bette Racki, Pat Chiles Schlabes, John Skarstad, and David Vaught were very helpful on many topics.

Photographs credited as "UC Davis Special Collections" are used by permission of the Department of Special Collections, University of California Library, Davis, California.

My most important debt is to Lyn H. Lofland. As spouse, friend, and colleague, she has wrestled each step of this project with me. I could not have carried it through without her unfailing help and support.

I have tried to make this book as accurate as possible. Nonetheless, it may still contain mistakes of typography and content. Therefore, it should not be taken as the only or definitive source on any topic.

A NOTE ON THE TEXT:
Bibliographical references are identified by parenthetic numbers throughout the text. These numbers correspond with the References section of this book (page 156).

INTRODUCTION

In this book, I offer a history of Davis, California, a village founded in 1868 that grew into a town in the early twentieth century and became a city later in the same century. Two features of the almost 14 decades of events at that place are especially striking. First, the ways of life there have changed radically. Second and at the same time, there have been many forms of continuity.

CHANGES AND CONSTANTS. Let me begin with an overview of these radical changes and deep constants.

    Changes: Nine Periods (and Communities?). The history of Davis takes place in a single location. But in some ways, it is difficult to say there was only one community there. Instead, the changes have been so profound that one might say there were a series of them. Reflecting the permutations and transformations of America itself, there may have been nine in succession, each a remaking of a previous community. Thus, there is no single "history" of Davis. There are many histories.

    The sequence of these nine provides the organizing principle of this book. Following an account of what was at Davis before there was a Davis, the following nine chapters are devoted to each of them. The nine can also be thought of as "periods" and clustered into three groups of three each under the headings village, town, and city.

- The first three tell of Davisville as a *village:* **1)** expectant congregation (1868–1871), **2)** wheat-growing shipping point (1872–1890), and **3)** almond cultivation center (1891–1904).
- The second three trace Davis's growth into a *town:* **4)** university farm locale (1905–1916), **5)** urbanizing municipality (1917–1929), and **6)** depression locality (1930–1945).
- The most recent three chronicle Davis becoming a *city:* **7)** exploding suburb (1946–1971), **8)** progressive community (1972–1989), and **9)** contested place (1990–).

These nine periods are also shown graphically and briefly characterized in the chart on page 65.

    Six of the nine years that start and end these periods were quite clear at the time and still are: *1868*, the Davisville grid was laid out and recorded; *1905*, the State Farm site search began; *1917*, Davis incorporated as a city and America entered World War I; *1929*, the American economy collapsed, also depressing

Davis; *1945*, World War II ended and a new world began; and *1972*, electoral revolt against "mindless" growth.

Three of the nine years were less dramatic than the six just listed. The changes they signify were important but took place more gradually. Each of these three is a plausible "midpoint" rather than a dramatic moment: *1872*, marking a shift from a boom and wealth mindset to expectations of a stable town; *1890*, indicating a gradual shift from "farming" to "cultivating" agriculture; and *1990*, signaling movement from a progressive to a contested Davis.

Changes: Civic Culture. There is a second way to think about changes. This is in terms of alternations of major themes in Davis's civic culture. Let me mention three of these here and elaborate on them at their points of change:

- *"We want Davis to Grow and Develop at a Significant Pace."* Up until the late 1960s or early 1970s, growth and development were unchanging—and unchallenged—dominant themes. But in the early 1970s, they became conflictful.
- *"Whatever is good for UC at Davis is good for Davis."* Although there were previous episodes of conflict, chronic disputes between "town" and "gown" began only in about the mid-1970s. These heavily focused on the town's complaint that the gown made plans and changes without informing the town and taking account of the effects on the town.
- *"We pretty much agree on who should serve on the City Council."* In chapters five through nine, I report the percentage of Davis voters in city council elections who cast ballots for the **1)** highest vote receiver and the **2)** lowest percent of votes that elected a candidate. Over 1918 to 2004, both percents fell very, very substantially. These declines signaled significant increases in political disagreements in Davis—or, a large increase in democracy.

Constants. Davis history is not an unrelieved story of change. Some things have been remarkably constant. These have included cultural themes such as:

- *"Shop at home. Patronize local merchants."*
- *"Davis has a severe housing shortage."*
- *"We are proud that Davis has a small town character."*
- *"We must maintain Davis's small town character."*
- *"We should (or are) improving the town by . . ."*

What's Featured and What's Not. Within the overarching themes of "radical changes, deep constants," certain topics are featured and others are not. Featured topics include population and growth, business and economics, politics, education, religion, the State Farm in its many incarnations, physical structures and infrastructure, and civic culture. In contrast, I do not report very much on such matters as athletics and organized sports, race and gender groups and their struggles, social service and welfare activities, medical practices, or crime and other deviance.

Introduction

Several circumstances explain this selectivity. One, this book was written with certain length restrictions. That being the case, I elected to do a few things in slight depth rather than a lot of things in no depth. Two, I have stood on the shoulders of my Davis history predecessors and used their contributions. Their works exhibit the selective foci just described. Three, my interests and previous work have been in these treated areas rather than in others.

I have written many books about human social life. But only now have I been overwhelmed with a sense of the severely selective and abbreviated nature of any story one tells. Not only do I slight the matters just indicated (and others), my reports on the topics I do feature are extraordinarily truncated. For the reasons just given, major and important aspects of virtually every topic I discuss have been left out. Such is a price we pay for saying anything.

One implication of this unavoidable truncation is that history is a process, not a product. Every told story is only a moment in a never-concluded process of telling.

BEFORE DAVIS. As we shall see in the next chapter, Davis grew like a mushroom patch. One day there was nothing much there; the next day there was a complex structure. Even so, Davis did not pop up entirely no-where and in a virgin land. Much was already in the immediate vicinity and a great deal had happened at that location in previous decades, centuries, and eons.

The Valley Environment. The Central Valley of California is some 450 miles long from above Redding on the north to below Bakersfield on the south. Before Americans profoundly reorganized it with one of the largest water control schemes in human history, the environment lurched year to year from drought to flood to Mediterranean-moderate climate. There was (and still is) no discernable pattern of year-to-year drought, flood, or moderate climate.

Before American recrafting, the valley floor was, with some frequency, an "inland sea" (6). This was a function of a simple but huge hydraulic in which the amount of winter rain and melted snow from the mountains exceeded the drainage capacity of the delta, the Carquinez Strait, and the San Francisco Bay. The result was backup and a large but temporary lake or "sea."

Short of an "inland sea," there could be serious flooding from the runoff of the Coastal Range toward the Sacramento River. *Floods* occurred in 1822, 1832, 1853, 1861–1862 (the "flood of the century"), 1868, 1869, 1871, 1872, 1895, and in later years. Conversely, *droughts* happened in 1856, 1857, 1863, 1864, 1865, 1870, and in later years (8, p. 11).

On top of these, infrequent but disastrous *frosts* coming at blossom-times could wipe out entire crops, as could *heat waves*. And, the dread *north wind* could dry out and kill crops.

Plant and Animal Life. There were, however, a sufficient number of moderate rain and snowfall years to allow the valley to develop considerable plant and animal life. Plant life on the valley floor was of two main kinds.

The channels where water ran in significant amounts down to what would be named the Sacramento River developed rich *riparian forests* along their banks. In what would become Yolo County, containing Davisville, there were two main channels from the Coastal Range to the Sacramento River. The northern channel is now called Cache Creek and the southern one, on which Davisville would be sited, is Putah Creek. Early observers reported that Putah Creek's riparian forests extended out upward of two miles on either side of it. But the Putah channel did not run all the way to the Sacramento River. Instead, its waters fanned out into a miles-wide lowland delta or basin that was a marsh in most years and which had developed into what was characterized as an "impenetrable thicket." This marsh/thicket began in the vicinity of what is now called El Macero (just southeast of Davis) and extended to the Sacramento River.

The riparian forest contained a variety of types of trees and plants, including oak, tule, cottonwood, grapevines, and wild roses. Abundant wildlife inhabited these forests, including beaver, deer, elk, coyote, wild cats, and the famous California grizzly bear.

The second type of plant life was *native grass* and it covered the great bulk of the valley floor in the moderate years. Early observers reported that one could see for many miles across what was, in many places, gently rolling countryside. Failed gold miners from the Midwest were struck with how these plains looked like home (27). (One ecologist has termed Yolo County "California Kansas.")

The First Humans. Apparently there was a time when people could and did walk across the Bering Strait from Asia to North America. They spread south and across the continent, some settling in the Central Valley and along Putah Creek. Organized as what anthropologists call "hunting and gathering" societies, the richness of the riparian forest provided for their survival.

By being semi-nomadic, these Native Americans, called the Patwin, could successfully adapt to droughts and floods (7, p. 6). In drought, they followed Putah Creek higher into the western mountains where water still flowed from underground springs and plant and animal life still flourished. In times of flood, they moved about the valley in boats made of tule reeds or likewise retreated to the mountains.

Thus, they moved among a number of settlement sites depending on the climate of the moment. One of these sites appears to have been in the vicinity of what are now called First and A Streets in Davis. At least, over several decades residents of that area have found a great many carved stone arrowheads lying on the ground or close to the surface. Some people theorize that the earth beneath the parking lot at the southeast corner of First and A Streets likely contains major artifacts remaining from a large Patwin encampment (8, p. 97).

As an isolated population, the Patwin had never been exposed to diseases such as malaria, measles, small pox, and gonorrhea. They had, therefore, not developed the resistance that comes from certain kinds of exposure. The arrival of Europeans and Americans in the early and middle 1800s spelled disaster. It is estimated that as much as three-quarters of the native population in the valley had died from disease epidemics by the time of the Gold Rush in

1849. When Davisville was founded in 1868, almost all these earliest inhabitants had been gone for at least 20 years.

Pre–Gold Rush Europeans and Mexicans. An assortment of European and American explorers, hunters, adventurers, and settlers ventured into the valley in the early 1800s. Early on, the Spanish and then the Mexicans laid claim to most of the land and divided it into large rancheros primarily used for grazing cattle.

The trappers were likely the most environmentally significant visitors. The riparian forests and streams had large numbers of fur-bearing animals, especially beaver. It was simple work to trap and kill them for the large, worldwide fur market. The hunters were so rapacious that by mid-century a number of species—especially beaver—were all but extinct.

John Sutter was the most famous of pre–Gold Rush Europeans. Although he was headquartered at his fort some 20 miles east of what would be Davisville, he and his people are reported to have come to Putah and Cache Creeks to cut down trees for lumber and fuel and to kill animals for pelts.

Gold Rush Failures. In the famous phrase, "the world rushed in" after 1849. While there were abundant miners, gold was abundant only briefly. Most people arrived too late to find gold without significant investment in machinery and scale of organization. Too embarrassed to have come a long way for little or nothing, these failed miners looked around for other ways to survive.

Many of them were from Midwestern farms and farms in other parts of the country. Looking at the expanse of open and virgin plain that was the valley, it was not hard to think that one could stay in California and farm. Indeed, one historian of this period, David Vaught (26, 27), has argued that in the mid-1800s there was a vast effort to recreate the Midwest in the California Central Valley.

By the 1860s, the years just before Davisville, there were already many farms of various sizes in Yolo and adjacent Solano Counties and several hundred people on them. The soil was so rich that in good rainfall years a great deal of money could be made, canceling out bank debt caused by bad weather. In addition, this was a period of poor wheat harvests in other parts of the world, making wheat-growing an especially lucrative activity (26, 27).

Jerome Davis was one of these Yolo farmers. He had developed what was for a time a prosperous and diverse agricultural enterprise on the north bank of Putah Creek. But like other farmers, the ravages of the weather created hard times for him. He mortgaged his holdings. One of those mortgages was bought by a company about to build a railroad from Vallejo to Sacramento.

The United States Acquired California. A great deal of this new farming was taking place on large, grazing rancheros. Some of these farmers thought they had legitimate grants allowing their activities. Others had less clear claims. In 1848, the United States took California from Mexico. This change raised questions about exactly who, if anyone, owned the land in the valley.

In the 1850s, the state was divided into counties and one of the early tasks of each county was internally to subdivide the land on a grid system using the concept of the township. In this process of exactly specifying plots and boundaries, a good deal of land trading went on, as well as much squatting on what were asserted to be previously unowned lands. Many years of litigation over ownerships ensued. Extending over a period of years, these disputes were eventually settled by hearings before, and the decrees of, the U.S. Land Commission.

Towns and Cities Near the Future Davisville. By the later 1860s, but still before Davisville was invented, Yolo and Solano Counties contained a considerable number of villages, towns, and even cities. Washington (now part of West Sacramento) was, in 1850, an early Yolo County seat. Flooding caused relocation to Cachville in 1857, other moves, and final relocation in Woodland in 1862. Founded in 1853, Woodland became the bustling center of agriculture in the county, even boasting two daily newspapers.

The Countryside. Out in the countryside, churches were going up, serving as social and religious centers for farm families. Although there was as yet no train, a dirt trail ran across the tules from Sacramento, next to what would be Davisville, and toward what would become Dixon, and on to Vallejo (an already well-established small city of some import).

At irregular intervals along this trail, entrepreneurs had constructed primitive horse stables, eating places, and overnight lodgings. One of these stopping places was just to the south of where a traveler forded Putah Creek and next to the site of the future Davisville. In what is now the UC Davis arboretum, this stopping place was called Solano House. It had stables and was a station on the route of the famous Pony Express (which was put out of business after 18 months by completion of the transcontinental telegraph in 1861).

Some accounts hold that before the Davisville grid was laid out in 1868, the former home of Jerome Davis—just southwest of what is today A and First Streets—had been turned into a hotel, general merchandise store, and saloon. There may also have been some nearby former farm buildings that housed an assortment of other activities and squatter residents.

* * *

These, then, were some of the features of the environment in which railroad entrepreneurs decided to build a train track. Along with buying the track right-of-way, they acquired adjacent lands on which to create towns and sell lots. The land of interest to us was the ranch just north of where the dirt trail crossed Putah Creek.

Chapter One

EXPECTANT DAVISVILLE, 1868–1871

At Vallejo in March of 1868, the California Pacific Railroad (the "Cal-P"), one of numerous new rail companies across the West, began laying tracks pointed toward the as yet nonexistent Davisville. At that future town, the single line would become two. One would continue east to Sacramento to meet the soon-to-arrive transcontinental railroad. The other would turn north to Woodland and on to Marysville (a major center once planned as the western terminus of the transcontinental railroad).

CONSTRUCTING THE RAILROAD. The track reached the new Davisville some six months later in late August or early September (depending on the account you accept). Over that period, people in Yolo and Solano Counties followed the project with great interest. The Woodland papers printed frequent reports on it and speculated excitedly about the growth and prosperity the train would bring. In particular, getting the tons of wheat out of Solano and Yolo Counties was a problem the train would solve. Bagged grain had to be hauled on horse-drawn wagons to Knight's Landing or Suisun in order to be loaded on boats. The railroad would mean much shorter trips and more frequent shipping. (In fact, the sidings built at Davis did become, for a time, a center for shipping wheat and other grain.)

In May, the editor of the *Yolo County Democrat* made a trip by "stage" (horse-drawn coach) to the site of the town-to-be and printed this report of what he saw:

> The road from [Woodland] . . . to Putah Creek passes over one of the richest portions of the county, and is skirted on either side by vast fields of grain which present a prospect of one of the most abundant and valuable harvests ever garnered in any part of the world. . . . At the crossing of Putah Creek, on the Solano side, a station is kept by J.H. Shuman, who, in company with enterprising citizens, is preparing to survey a plot for the depot of the Solano and Yolo Railroad . . . . The prospective settlement is, we believe, to be called "Veranda City" (*Democrat*, May 30, 1868).

The July 4 *Democrat* described progress:

> The proposed location of the depot of the Vallejo Railroad, on Putah Creek, is now being laid off in lots, and a town of considerable importance will soon spring up in that locality. The site is on the

bank of Putah Creek, at Davis' ranch, in a healthy and rich agricultural district settled by farmers most of who have secured a competence to themselves as the reward of their energy and frugality. A large store is already in process of erection and will be completed and furnished with new goods in a few days, by the proprietor, Wm Dresbach, who is well known to the community as a gentleman of superior business and attainments and social qualities. The hotel there is thronged with visitors attracted by the promising business character of the place. The new town is to be called Davisville (*Democrat*, July 4, 1868).

Sources disagree on exactly when the tracks (and train) actually reached the new depot at Davisville. Some report August 24, others say September 8 or so. The *Democrat* of September 5 stated that the "road has been completed as far as Putah Creek. A bridge will be immediately constructed across that stream and in a few days the locomotive will make its first appearance in Yolo County."

For about three months, Davisville was the "end of the line." But the Cal-P pressed on and the *Democrat* of November 14 announced the following:

CONNECTION COMPLETE—The track of the California Pacific Railroad has been laid down between Davisville and Washington [now merged into West Sacramento], thus making the connection by rail complete between Vallejo and Washington. The first train passed over the new road on Tuesday evening last [November 10]. . . .

CREATING DAVISVILLE. The "Big Five" owners of the Cal-P had nineteenth-century names reminiscent of a Dickens novel: John B. Frisbie, DeWitt C. Haskin, DeWitt C. Rice, William F. Roelofson, and James M. Ryder. In addition to building a railroad, these five were land speculators and developers. As part of their railroad plan, they bought a mortgage on the southern portion of the Davis farm, which had fallen on hard times because of drought and flooding, on November 1, 1867. Davis defaulted on payment in 1868 and the Cal-P came to control much of the mortgaged part of the farm. Constituting themselves a separate entity called the Davisville Land Company, 200 acres were transferred to it, the Davis family having left the farm some years before. Many of its structures were the initial buildings of Davisville, although they were outside the grid of blocks named Davisville (and are seen in the bottom portion of the picture on page 66).

The 32-block grid shown in the picture on page 66 is reported to have been conceived and sketched by the Davisville Land Company president, Dr. DeWitt Rice (a pharmacist). For historical context I should report that inventing towns composed of ad hoc grids connected to new railroads was very common across the Midwest and West in this period. Thousands of towns began in this fashion. Davisville was a typical "paper town."

Newspaper reports suggest that blocks and lots were staked out and buildings constructed as early as May. However, the plat was not officially recorded until November 28, 1868.

EXPECTANT DAVISVILLE. The quote from the July 4 *Democrat* just above begins to convey the atmosphere that prevailed at the new Davisville. Judging from the reports of nearby newspapers and in the *Davis Advertiser* (published weekly from December 4, 1869, to May 7, 1870), the ethos was one of "big things are going to happen." People were in on the ground floor of a future big (and rich) town.

Nineteenth-Century Booms and Davisvillle. This belief becomes more understandable when we know that recently founded towns that were the scenes of rapid growth and new fortunes occurred with some frequency in nineteenth-century America. The city of Chicago was the prototypical example. From frontier outpost, it had rapidly become an urban giant and the producer of many fortunes. Who could be certain where the next one would be? Why not Davisville? After all, it was at the junction of major east-west and north-south railroads. In a matter of a few months in 1868 and 1869, at least 500 people had arrived and begun to make a town. From open land, virtually overnight this was already a small but bustling center made all the more lively by frequent trains and large-scale grain shipping.

The pages of the *Davisville Advertiser* portrayed this Davisville in 1869 and 1870. Here is a montage of items that suggest how these first Davisites might reasonably have formed expectations of imminent growth and fortune. I begin with a sketch of Davis written by the *Advertiser* editors Orr and Bonham, published on December 4, 1869. This date was about a year and a half after people began congregating at this new town:

> At the present time of writing Davisville has a voting population of nearly 400. Up to the present time, there have been 200 houses built. We have our hotels, drug stores, hardware, dry goods, and clothing stores; post office and express office, liquor stores, livery stables, blacksmith, wagon making, carpenter and furniture shop; meat markets, and in fact everything of that kind a town should have.
>
> Several different religious denominations hold services here on the Sabbath, whilst our public school is in a most flourishing condition.
>
> Davisvillle, situated as it is in one of the largest agricultural districts in the State, will in the future assume a population and wealth to rank it second to none on the coast. Its railroad advantages give it now predominance over other places; with its two railroads converging here, and the third a fixed fact, why should it not prosper?
>
> To any of our readers in the Eastern States, or on this coast, desirous of investing their money in town property that will double itself in a short time, we would say visit Davisville and judge for yourselves the truth of our remarks.

Life in Expectant Davisville. Although an expectation of prosperity seems to have been the overarching mindset, there were many ordinary aspirations and activities.

Perusing the *Advertiser*'s advertisements, one found a lively range of business activity. There were the expected livery stables, dentists, liquor merchants, wagon makers, and the like. One also found some goods and services less expected on the western frontier:

> Mrs. Bryant will take a few pupils for instruction on the piano. Those desirous of learning will do well to call, as she is a lady fully competent to teach. Tuition, $8 per month.

* * *

> **Fashionable Dressmakers**
> Olive Street, Davisville
> Mrs. GROSCUP and Miss FLIGGLE
> Have now rooms in Dr. Lane's building
> And are prepared to do all kinds of
> Plain and Fancy Needle Work,
> CUTTING AND FITTING OF DRESSES,
> TRIMMING HATS, ETC.

* * *

> Miss Louie M. Brown will give instructions in the Art of Spencerian pennmanship at the schoolhouse, commencing on Tuesday eve. Jan. 25. Tuition, for fifteen lessons, $5, stationary included. All are invited.

* * *

> Mrs. C.M. Stowe, trance medium, is in the city and will give a lecture at Clark's Hall on Sunday eve, March 6; a collection will be taken up after the lecture to defray the expenses of the lady. . . . "Having directed her mental vision toward the curing of disease, she clearly sees it, and that of the medical agents required." She can be consulted at the American Hotel, room 5 from 9 A.M. to 9 P. M., for a few days.

From virtually the first issue, *Advertiser* editors and advertisers enunciated the *shop locally* theme that would become one of strongest and frequently repeated elements of Davis civic life. If ever there was a clear example of an eternal verity (at least in the sense of an incessantly harped-on idea), it is surely the admonition to "shop at home." Here is an editorial version of it in the March 12, 1870, *Advertiser*:

> One of the means by which we may build up a place, neighborhood or county, and bring prosperity to our business generally, is for everyone to patronize home institutions, especially in articles that are manufactured there. Keep the money circulating in your neighborhood is the way to make it rich, and every man that sends away for work that he can just as easily get done at home deprives the place of just that wealth, as well as discourages enterprises.

Chapter One: Expectant Davisville, 1868–1871

Significant numbers of people who were strangers to one another were congregating at this new place called Davisville. The basis on which they might relate to one another aside from sheer commercial transactions was problematic. At some other new places, family, religion, and/or ethnicity often provided a universe of commonality and discourse that facilitated social life, conviviality, and order beyond commercial and political relations.

But the people congregated at Davisville did not appear to have been strongly bound together in family, religious, national, or ethnic ways (although some shared a religion—Catholicism, Presbyterianism, or Methodism). The number of people representing any of these non-economic/non-political relationships seemed below the numbers needed to crystallize much organized social life.

Apparently providing such broader relations, *lodges* were very active almost from the first days of the village. Consider these *Davis Advertiser* reports of early and widespread programs.

> The Good Templar lodge is in a very flourishing condition, having initiated eight more members last Saturday night—making in all 51 members.
>
> * * *
>
> Guiding Star Lodge No. 361 I.O.G.T. gave a public installation of officers on Friday night the 4th. . . . after the initiatory ceremonies— five being initiated, making in all 62 . . . they returned to the hall and hopped away the hours of the night . . . .
>
> * * *
>
> On Tuesday evening, April 12 there will be instituted in this place a Lodge of the Independent Order of the Odd Fellows.
>
> * * *
>
> The First Annual picnic Excursion of Siskyou Tribe No. 19, Davisville, will take place at Tammany Park [aka Grove], St Tammany's Day, Thursday May 12th, 1870. Members of the Order at Vallejo, Marysville, Sacramento and other points . . . are invited. Ladies, gentlemen and children. . are assured that perfect order will be maintained during the day. Arrangements have been made with the California Pacific R.R. to issue Excursion tickets at half fare for the Vallejo and Marysville routes. A special train will be waiting at the Vallejo Depot, Sacramento to convey the Citizens of Sacramento to and from the Park. . . A first class band has been secured. The dancing floor is [in] excellent condition. Every effort has been taken to make this the Pow Wow of the season. Everyone who wishes to see the Indian war dance will be present.

As this last item suggests, lodge events were a significant element of social life in the Central Valley, not only in Davisville. Tammany Grove (or Park) was a picnic grounds established in 1870 by the Improved Order of Red Men in a "fine oak grove" about a mile north of Davisville. An *Advertiser* story described it as a "dance hall 50x100, with all the necessary dressing rooms, etc. for the ladies, the floor is elevated 10 feet above the ground, and enclosed. [There are] also ample seats throughout the ground, clear, clean water and the cars of the Cal. Pa. R.R. run by it. The Tribe have spared no means to make this the best place of resort in the State."

Hard drinking and saloons were an important feature of the male-dominated frontier west. As the gender ratio began to equalize in new towns such as Davisville, there remained the problem of social life to compete with saloon life. One suggestion is that some lodges provided settings of conviviality outside saloons in particular and drinking in general. Consider this letter to the *Advertiser* editors:

> EDITOR ADVERTISER—I notice in the columns of your last issue that a Lodge of the I.O.G.T's has been established in your burg. Well, I am pleased to hear of any move to advance real happiness in our land. Intemperance is an evil that ever preys on its victim's mind and lures him on to misery and death.

Establishing a public school was among the first acts of citizens at the new Davisville. Enthusiasm and pride over the local school is evident in this report:

> On last Friday our public school took a vacation for one week to allow both teachers and pupils an opportunity to recuperate for the Spring term. Under the skillful management of Prof. Shellhous, our public school has acquired a reputation second to none in the State, and we challenge any public school in the State to compete it in any of its educational branches.

Raising funds for schools was (and is) a perennial and unending community effort.

> **Benefit Wednesday Night** was a grand success, there being $50 taken in, all of which goes to pay off our school indebtedness. The audience was an appreciative one, as was fully demonstrated by the loud and prolonged cheering . . . The public school of this place will ever be indebted to Dr. E.J. Shellhous for the liberal spirit manifested by him towards it.

By April of 1870, the Davisville school had two teachers and an enrollment of 50 students, with 36 in the "Primary Department."

That month, the public school "gave an exhibition at Philliber's Hall." The program, printed on the front page of the April 7, 1870, *Advertiser*, began with a "Greeting Song" sung by the entire school and proceeded through four types of performances:

> **Declamation**, four of them by four different students.
> **Dialogue**, ten of them by several students each, on such topics as "Disease of My Punctuation," "When Doctors Disagree," "Who Shall Decide," "The Pedagogue in Trouble," and "My Grammar Class."
> **Speech,** one of them.
> **Song,** three of them by the entire student body, including the songs "Our Beautiful Flag," and "Good Night."

In this same period, people began to feel that the rented building in which the school was conducted was too crowded, small, and uncomfortable. A campaign to raise funds for a school building ensued. What was now called the "Town Company," which still owned many Davisville lots, agreed to "donate a tract of land in size sufficient for school buildings and playgrounds and subscribe in money liberally toward the building, if the citizens will take hold of the matter and erect a No. 1 school building" (1, March 9, 1870). A vote on this proposition was held on April 25, 1870. It passed and a two-story schoolhouse was erected on six lots donated by the Town Company that same year. (The lots were in the block bounded by B-C and Third-Fourth.)

Expectant Davisville was definitely run by men. Although some operators of businesses were clearly women (see the examples given above), business people were written of as "he," "him," and "his." Nevertheless, gender equality had become an issue, especially regarding the right to vote.

> **Enfranchisement of Women**
> On Tuesday evening Mrs. M. Fields lectured at Clark's Hall on the above subject, to a large and enthusiastic audience of ladies and gentlemen. She handled the subject in a masterly manner, and depicted to her listeners the amount of misery that would be brought upon the human race, the disgrace that would befall the daughters of Eve, should they secure the right to vote. On the whole, we think, the lecture was one of eloquence and common sense (1, March 12, 1870).

Each issue of the *Advertiser* contained columns of what were called "Left Letters." The issue of April 2, 1870, for example, had "ninety-eight in the post office and forty in the express." This was the count of one "J.O.N." who wrote a weekly "Davisville Doings" column for the *Woodland Daily Democrat* in 1897. In January of that year, someone gave him a copy of the April 2, 1870, issue of the *Advertiser* and he remarked that these numbers were "fairly indicative of the transient nature" of the Davisville population. He went on to opine about Davisville in 1870:

> Hundreds were coming and going. A few remained, but even these were too busy to look after their letters. Davisville was then a lively

town with bright prospects, but in common with many another it has gone backward since. Then it supported the Advertiser, two doctors, two dentists, a restaurant, two hotels, half a dozen saloons, as many stores, and one resident lawyer. Now it scarcely supports itself (*Woodland Daily Democrat*, January 4, 1897).

Growth and Improvement. Let us return to the topic of expectations of fortune at Davisville. The proprietors of the *Advertiser* seemed to have made every effort to report any sign of growth and improvement that came to their attention and to use such examples as vehicles for exhorting emulation:

> A number of our citizens have already planted trees in front of their dwelling houses and places of business. This is right and we hope to see our streets lined with them, for there is nothing a person can do that will so beautify a place or make it seem more like *home* than to have trees and shrubbery around . . . The sides of our streets lined with shade trees . . . would give our town a very picturesque appearance, and at the same time it would be inviting to strangers who visit us to come again.
>
> *   *   *
>
> Our citizens have become aroused at last, for from the depot to Mr. Dresbach's store they are laying a plank walk, and also, one will soon be commenced from the depot to this part of the town. The crossing to the post office on Olive street is completed; Gentleman, we, in behalf of the ladies, thank you.

Some people clearly were not satisfied with such examples. In the February 19, 1870, *Advertiser* the editors felt it necessary to reply to the allegation that Davisville was dead:

> Who dare say Davisville is dead, that there is not any improvement visible. Morgan has commenced to build a residence on the corner of Oak and First streets, which will be, when finished, an ornament to our town; and between Mr. Haight's drug store and Mr. Philliber's restaurant there is another house going up, intended, we believe, for a saloon. Across the railroad a gentleman has finished a house; Mr. Philliber has planted a lot of very large and handsome trees in front of his restaurant, and First street shows visible changes. On the whole we think that is enough to convince the most skeptical that the burg is on the improve, and that this will be a Spring of improvements.

To say that expectations for growth were dimming and that, in historical perspective, a boom did not happen is not to say there were no improvements.

Among others like those the editors mention above, in 1871 the original eight by four-block grid was enlarged on its eastern edge. Another tier of blocks was added, creating what is now L Street. An additional tier of blocks was also added on the north, creating what is now Sixth Street. As the first and for a time the only railroad station in Yolo County, Davisville quickly became the local shipping center. In a short history of the village published in 1900, William Henry Scott claimed that "during that first year [1868–1869] from fourteen to twenty thousand tons of wheat were shipped from here" (25, p. 8). The railroad was subsequently completed though Woodland and Knights Landing. These new shipping points "deprived Davisville of a large proportion of the freight and business that before had been tributary to it" (25, p. 9).

Disillusion Confessed. Even though there were improvements, there was also clearly no boom or any reason to think one might start.

Near the end of the six-month run of the *Advertiser*, on March 12, 1870, Orr and Bonham came to this realization. Rather than exuberance, they expressed disillusionment. Further, they blamed large land owners for the recent slackening of immigration and growth.

> We are told every day that it is necessary to do considerable blowing for Davisville. Now we would like to know what is the use? . . . . The citizens of our town are willing to do all they can to induce immigration, but let the citizens outside hold out some inducement; and our Legislature put a tax on these heavy land holders equal to the value of their property and they will be glad to sell. If we are the lucky owners of a 50x120 we could be compelled to pay taxes to its full valuation; whilst our neighbor Jones, owns 20,000 acres and he is assessed at *thirty cents an acre*! And as long as this is the case, so long will our changes be slim for an increase of population.
>
> Davisville is admitted by all to be the very Eden of California; to be the finest wheat growing, wine producing, stock raising portion of the state, but as long as a few own all the land everything will remain as it is.

A Village Too Small. Almost two months after publishing the above confession of disillusion, Orr and Bonham threw in the towel. Declaring May 7, 1870, to be the date of their final issue, they wrote bitterly about Davisville's lack of support. One problem was the amount of advertiser and reader patronage. While these were not entirely adequate, the even larger problem was that the prospects for growth and new support were not good. Here is how they ended their venture:

VALEDICTORY

We are done. We have written the last line! We have pressed the last sheet! Our pilgrimage is o'er. None had done more for the prosperity of Davisville than us; and none have done less to help than you. We are through! *Vale!*

WILL ORR.

To those of our patrons who have come forward and helped us in our days of want we thank you; to those who promised to and held aloof, you can thank yourselves. For six months night and day we toiled and struggled on promises, but promises wouldn't pay board bills . . . . Corporations had promised to help us, in case we needed it, but when we asked them for it, they quietly told us to burst.

But we have friends here, good, true friends. They would gladly have come forward to our help, but we did not wish to involve them.

ORR & BONHAM (1, May 7, 1870)

* * *

There would be at least three more unsuccessful efforts to publish a newspaper in Davisville before, finally, in 1898 (28 years after the *Advertiser's* demise), the *Davisville Enterprise* succeeded. The first effort, *The Facts*, was published from January 29 to September 2, 1878 (25, January 12, 1900). The second, the *Signal* "published intermittently in the 1880s" (7, p. 110). And the third, a second *Advertiser*, appeared briefly in 1892. Its editor commented "one would have to live off the labels of tomato cans to run a paper in Davisville" (7, p. 110). Unfortunately, not even a single issue of any of these three papers is known to have survived. This 28-year gap means that it is more than ordinarily difficult to glimpse Davisville between 1870 and 1898.

Chapter Two

FARMING DAVISVILLE, 1872–1890

Exuberant hopes of rapid growth and riches faded and residents settled into the idea of Davisville as a farm-centric village. Disillusioned "boomists" left town or at least dropped out of public life. New people arrived.

This stable (or perhaps declining) Davisville would last some 33 years, from about 1872 to1904. These 33 years divide in a general way into periods of the predominance and decline of "farming" agriculture and a period of the increase in "cultivating" agriculture.

FARMING VERSUS CULTIVATING. At the level of technique, *farming* agriculture refers to plowing open plains in the fall or winter, planting wheat, barley, or other grains, and expecting the winter rains to produce the crop. Seen narrowly, this is "dry crop" farming, meaning that the farmer does not irrigate. *Cultivating* agriculture involves plants that must be tended (cultivated) and irrigated year after year. Near Davis, such plants included almond trees and grapevines. People engaged in this second activity are sometimes called orchardists, growers, or horticulturalists rather than farmers (26, p, 14; 27). Moreover, this distinction often refers to differences in broader approaches to agriculture and not only to differences in technique (26, ch. 1).

From the 1850s to the 1910s, farming gradually decreased in emphasis while cultivating gradually increased. I have selected 1890 as the year in which the two crossed. Other students of this history might reasonably select a year before or after this one. But before the 1890s, "dryland cereal grains—barley, oats, and wheat" were the order of the day. "By 1875 nearly 200,000 acres [of them] were in cultivation across the region" (24, p. 6).

Factors that encouraged a "California 'wheat boom' of the 1880s," of which Davisville was very much a part, included the presence of "farmer-engineers" (24, p. 6). These were farmers "with a mechanical bent, who invented or helped design mule-drawn machines that literally marched across wheat fields like an army" (24, p. 6). (One is shown on page 67.)

Nevertheless, dry farming declined and for at least five reasons. First, such farming was at the mercy of flood and drought. One could become wealthy in a good year or years; one could also be wiped out in a bad year. Not infrequent flood and drought years also made it prudent to grow crops with more predictable yields (e.g. almonds). Second, in the 1850s, wheat and other grains were growing on virgin soil of very high fertility. By the 1880s, these lands were still productive, but not as productive. But the same process of exceptionally high yields on virgin land was then being repeated further north in Oregon and Washington. Yolo farmers were competing against them now with lower yields. Third, Central Valley wheat was marketed at good prices worldwide because crops abroad had been poor. As wheat yields improved elsewhere, prices dropped, prompting shifts to other crops. Most pointedly, the wheat market crashed in 1887, making production very problematic. Fourth, the new nationwide railroads combined with new refrigeration technology made it possible to transport fragile foodstuffs to distant markets. Items such as apples, peaches, and lettuce became parts of the diets of far-off urban dwellers. Lastly, there were cultural shifts in conceptions of the "healthy diet," which expanded the market for foodstuffs beyond grains such as wheat. Of special relevance to Davis history, before the late 1800s the almond was considered an exotic item and consumed by a small portion of the population. But by the early 1900s, the almond, along with some other food items, had become virtual health foods. Almonds, therefore, became a major Davis product in part because the market for them expanded.

ECONOMIC STRUCTURE IN 1880. In the late 1870s, L.M. McKenney undertook to compile and publish what he titled *McKenney's District Directory for 1879–80 of Sacramento . . . and Yolo Counties, Including all Residents, with Sketch of Cities and Towns.* The title page went on to inform us that "every RESIDENT AND LAND-OWNER in these . . . counties appears with the Number of Acres and Postoffice Address."

The entry on Davisville was in two parts, a brief textual sketch and a list of people. The textual sketch read, in part:

> The society of the place is above the average, so far as morality and refined culture are concerned. The business men are enterprising and keen-witted, and the town justly claims a "full compliment" of handsome ladies.
>
> There are three pretty churches, which represent the Catholic, Methodist and Presbyterian denominations, several nice residences and two hotels—the Gafford House, conducted on the European plan, being a most desirable haven for the weary traveler. Its kind and generous-hearted host, J.W. Gafford, Esq., never fails to inspire feelings of confidence, in his honesty of purpose in the breasts of his guests.
>
> The natural advantages of the place warrant a steady increase in its size. The farmers, as a class, are industrious and "well off" in the vicinity, and their beautiful fields of grain, regularly laid off orchards and well constructed homes show a spirit that deserves to be applauded. It has a population of 400 people.

A list of 196 people said to be "Davisville" followed this sketch. An occupation was given for each person. Ninety-two were labeled farmers, which meant that the great bulk of them were likely not residents of Davisville in the narrow sense of actually living in the village. Even so, McKenney considered them Davisville. That leaves about 100 on the list who actually lived in the town. Since McKenney also claimed the population of the town was 400, this meant that at least 300 residents of the village were not listed. Who might they be? Two probable categories of them are women and children. For McKenney, these people (with a few exceptions) were not sufficiently Davisville to be listed.

This brings us to the inference that the 196 people listed are those that McKenney and his surveyors thought were the *important people* of the Davisville area. They were the people he did not want to offend by leaving them out (lest they not buy his book, which sold for the not-small sum of $3).

Therefore, knowing who is *on* the list provides important information about the economic and social organization of Davisville in 1880. What do we see? As said, occupations are reported for all 196 (including an occupation reported as "widow"). I have grouped the occupations into ten categories of types of economic activity. These can be regarded as making up the village economy. Ordered from the most to the least frequent, these categories are as shown:

	(Percent) (number)
Farmers:	**47** (92)
Town Services:	**19** (38) (*One of each*: barber, hardware, upholsterer, drayman, baker, druggist, dressmaker, teamster, physician, cook, produce dealer, waiter, liquor dealer, constable, justice of the peace, laundry, boardinghouse. *Two of each*: baker, hotel operator, boot maker. *Four of each*: clergyman, retail store. *Eight*: saloon.)
Laborers:	**10** (19)
Business Services:	**6** (12) (*Four of each*: bookkeeper. *Eight*: clerk.)
Horse-Related:	**6** (12) (*One*: livery stable. *Two*: Carriage or wagon maker. *Eight*: blacksmith.)
Building:	**5** (9) (*One*: lumber. *Four*: carpenter. *Four*: painter.)
Railroad-Related:	**3** (6)
Crop Dealers:	**2** (5) (*One*: fruit. *Two*: grain. *Three*: cattle.)
Manufacturing:	**1** (2) (*One of each*: brewery, derricks.)
Other:	**0** (1) (*One*: widow.)
Total	**99%** (196) (less than 100% because of rounding)

Several features of this economy are of note. (1) A large part of it produced wealth as distinct from providing a service. (2) These wealth-producers were overwhelmingly farmers. Other creators of wealth were quite small (one brewery and one small manufacturer of derricks). (3) Important portions of the village economy provided services for farmers: horse-related (6 percent), business services, especially bookkeepers (6 percent), railroad related (6 percent), and crop dealers (2 percent). (4) What is often called the "service sector" of the economy was rather small, with only one, two, or a few practitioners of most services. (5) A number of services seem not to be present, such as attorneys, schoolteachers, bankers, and undertakers. My surmise, however, is that at least some of these were actually in Davisville, but McKenney did not think they were important enough to put on the list. These and other services were also available in the much larger and nearby town of Woodland and city of Sacramento. (6) The number eight given for saloons means that eight people reported their occupations as "saloon." This may or may not mean that they owned and operated an independent saloon as opposed to being employed by one. However, the Sanborn Fire Insurance map of Davisville for 1888 (the earliest known Sanborn for Davisville) shows nine saloons. (The next Sanborn, that for 1891, shows eight saloons.)

FARMERS AND DAVISVILLE. McKenney's list performs the important service of communicating to us the possibility (and I think the reality) that the farmers surrounding Davisville were very much involved in the village even though relatively few of them lived in it. They were de facto residents by virtue of their participation in churches, lodges, selling food to stores, dealings with crop dealers, and servicing by blacksmiths and other horse-related concerns. Certainly not least, they bought ordinary goods and services such as groceries, clothes, and lumber and other building supplies.

It is important to provide some texture to this generalization about the close interconnection of farmers and Davisville. One of the best ways to do this is by means of selections from an extraordinary diary kept from 1888 to 1928 by Davisville farmer and cultivator George Washington Pierce the younger. His farm was some five miles west of Davis, between Putah Creek and what is now called Russell Boulevard. His father—also named George Washington Pierce—had established and operated it from the 1850s to 1888, when he retired and moved into Davisville.

The younger George was born in 1850, was age 18 when Davisville was founded, and attended the University of California in Berkeley. Graduating in 1875, he was the first Central Valley person to earn a degree from the University of California. He had planned to become an attorney, but his father's failing health prompted him to return home and operate the ranch.

The extensive Pierce family papers, including the almost forty volumes of his diary, were donated to the Special Collections department of the University Library at UC Davis. Handwritten, they were transcribed by Professor of History Emeritus Richard N. Schwab.

These extracts are selected to show the *varied nature* and the *high frequency* of his trips back and forth between his ranch and Davisville.

Sat 7 Apr 1888.   Went to Davisville with one of the mares to Mullers. Attended Lodge at Davisville this evening

Sun 8 Apr 1888.	Mrs. Pierce and Self attended church at Davisville
Tues 18 July 1888.	Went to Davisville this forenoon to see about selling wheat can get a little over $1.25
Tues 6 Nov 1888.	Presidential election day. Susie and I went to town. Took pies cakes butter cream milk & bisquit for the election dinner to be given by the Presbyterian ladies.
Tues 26 Nov 1888.	Went to town and hired another man, Marin— to drive team.
Sat 23 Mar 1889.	Went to town with 4 mules & 2 wagons—took 30 doz eggs—got 50 posts 40–24ft & 10–16ft fencing. Lee worked on fence.
Mon 25 Mar 1889.	Went to town with span of mules - got lumber, salt, nails beans paint mustard sauce &c.
Sat 18 May 1889.	Went to Davis—got screens & trough & new copper teakettle. oranges berries &c–
Sat 1 June 1889.	Went to town in afternoon with Alfred got 5000 grain bags of Stelling @ 8c and 2 bales twine—got lumber to make harness room raspberries, cherries oil can meal pearl barley &c–
Mon 10 June 1889.	Tauzers men I was to have help me today got drunk yesterday and were run away with. Went to town got two men to rush[?] haying.

HENRY WILLIAMS ON DAVISVILLE IN 1877. Because Davisville did not have a newspaper most years before 1898, we are more than ordinarily dependent on travelers and other outside commentators to give us a glimpse of local life. One of these is provided by Henry T. Williams, publisher and editor of *The Pacific Tourist: An Illustrated Trans-Continental Guide*, published in New York in 1877. Mr. William offers these observations on Davisville in the late 1870s.

> Davisville . . . has a population of 300 . . . and two stores, a dozen saloons, four restaurants, and a Presbyterian, a Methodist Episcopal, and a Roman Catholic Church. About the same proportion of saloons to the population holds good over California, but that of the churches does not. But "Davisville is not an immoral place, for the liquor is all sold to *non-residents*."
>
> In 1862 land was worth from $6 to $10 per acre, and now sells at $75 to $100.
>
> Near Davisville are large orchards, "Briggs" covering 400 acres, and the "Silk Ranche" orchard 250 acres, but in dry seasons the quantity and quality of the fruit is greatly impaired by the want of irrigation.
>
> The failure of silk culture was largely owing to the hot winds from the north, killing the worms.

"Silk culture" refers to the thousands of mulberry trees I.N. Hoag planted near Davisville in 1869. He bought silkworm eggs with the plan that they would eat mulberry leaves after hatching, a step in the process of making silk. Unfortunately, the temperature was above 100 degrees ten days running in 1871, which killed the worms.

GRAIN WAREHOUSES. Farming had a major impact on the physical appearance of Davisville. In the same way a college cannot but loom large in a town, local farmers put their physical stamp on the village.

This took of the form of eight or so large warehouses for storing bags of wheat and other grain prior to loading them on trains. The railroad tracks between Third and Sixth Streets were almost solidly lined with these structures. A sense of this is conveyed in the picture on page 69, which is a photo reproduced from a postcard that featured them.

Grain was sold by weight, which therefore required a means of weighing. There were at least two large scales onto which farmers pulled wagons to be weighed. One of these was at the northeast corner of G and Fifth Streets, the site of the current Hibbert Lumber. The scale and the building from which it was operated are shown in the picture on page 68. Another scale was at the southeast corner of Fourth and G Streets. Legend has it that the scale was never removed and the current building there sits on it.

CHURCHES. As Henry Williams mentions just above, Davisville early on had three churches. St. James Catholic Church was constructed at the northeast corner of Third and I Streets in 1875 (and burned in 1933). That same year, the Methodists built a church at the northwest corner of Third and E Streets. The building was removed or dismantled some years later (the historical facts are in dispute) and the congregation disbanded.

Prior to both these, the numerically dominant Presbyterians built a church at the northeast corner of Fourth and E Streets in 1870. We know a little about the Presbyterians in this period because the group kept a *Minutes of the Session and Register of Communicants* starting on November 13, 1873. Written in longhand, Clare L. Childers transcribed and indexed them in 1997 and they were published by the Yolo County Historical Society. Here are two excerpts, both written by J.B. Tufts, clerk of sessions, which hopefully convey the texture of the Presbyterian form of Davisville religious life:

> *March 17, 1883*. Session met at the house of Elder J.B. Tufts. . . .
> Wiliam F. Tufts appeared before the session and made confession, that he had not lived and acted as a Christian ought, and was sorry for it. And asked forgiveness of the Church—and stated that he felt that God had forgiven him—and that he desired and now proposed by His help to live a consistent and useful Christian life. . . .
>
> *Sunday, March 18, 1883*. After sermon by the Rev. J.E. Anderson the Sacrament of the Holy Communion was administered to about fifty persons and the morning exercise closed with a crowded house and

one of the most solemn and affecting scenes ever witnessed in our Church. The spirit of our Lord was present in a marked degree and was plainly visibly [*sic*] to all (21, pp. 26–27).

THE DRINK DEMON, LODGES, AND THE WCTU. The lodges described in the last chapter as vigorous in the initial years of Davisville appear to have continued their strength. Here is a report from the Woodland *Yolo Democrat* of December 11, 1879:

> The second quarterly meeting of the sixth year of the Yolo County Good Templars was held at Davisville, November 28 and 29. . . The members of Orion No. 224 entertained the audience with recitations, tableaux, singing, and closed with the lively comedy of "We are all Teetotalers," which was well rendered, to the great amusement of the audience. . . .
>
> Sister E.P. Stevens, of San Francisco, held her listeners in rapt attention as she spread before her audience the terrible evils of the drink demon. The time passed only too rapidly with such pleasant surroundings . . .

Although the temperance lodges seemed to have many members, the Woman's Christian Temperance Union (WCTU), formed in 1888, struggled. It had few members, business meetings that lacked quorums, and months at a time without meetings. We know this, or can infer it, because the group kept minutes that have survived in the vault of the Davis Community Church. Written in longhand, Clare L. Childers transcribed them for publication by the Yolo County Historical Society. Taken by Mrs. Hortense Rowland, secretary, here are excerpts that convey something of the group's travails:

> *Nov. 28, 1888.* The Davisvillle W.C.T.U. met at 2 o-clock at Mrs. Hampton's. The meeting was opened by song "Who-so-Ever-Will" and prayer by the Pres. The 146th Psalm was read. . . . It was ordered by the President that a boy be placed in the Depot for the purpose of holding temperance and religious literature for the benefit of the public. Mrs. Rowland was appointed to secure the boy. [There is no further mention of this plan.]

> *Jan. 9, 1889.* The Committee on placing a paper holder at the depot, reported that the R.R. Supt. refused to let it be put up, considering it an advertisement. . . . The committee . . . was granted further time . . . to wait on the Supt. and see if the decision could not be changed.

> *June 5, 1889.* A meeting of the W.C.T.U. was held in the [Methodist] church June 5. Present three . . . Talks were had on various subjects of interest to the Union. . . . After regrets at the lack of interest and encouraging talk the meeting closed with singing (29, pp. 12–13).

THE ROAD TO WINTERS AND THE AVENUE OF THE TREES.

When ranches were first plotted between Davisville and Winters, there was no road. To travel to Davisville from the west, one had to cross the property of other people. The difficulty of travel—especially moving wheat and other products to the train in Davisville—made it clear that public roads were needed. In 1874, eighteen residents west of Davisville petitioned the Yolo County Board of Supervisors to create a road between Davis and Winters. (The Davis part of it is now named Russell Boulevard.) The 19th owner whose property the proposed road crossed refused to give the required land. The supervisors condemned it and took it from him. The road was opened on September 4, 1874 (8, p. 101).

Bare dirt roads became rutted and uneven, a problem to which the county responded with a road-grading program begun in 1876. The road thus stabilized, the LaRue family began to plant the rows of Black Walnuts still seen along about 2 miles of the road in what is now far west Davis. These trees have since come to be called "The Avenue of the Trees" and have been designated a City of Davis Historic Resource.

* * *

This was the last period in which humans and horses were prime sources of power. Petroleum- and electrically-driven devices appear in the next period and lead to radical increases in the scale and consequences of agricultural and other human activities.

Chapter Three

CULTIVATING DAVISVILLE, 1891–1904

For reasons enumerated at the beginning of the previous chapter, Davisville agriculturists expanded from "farmed" to "cultivated" crops—from dry/grain crops to irrigated/specialty crops. This chapter is about that expansion over the years 1891 to 1904 and about other aspects of the village.

CULTIVATING EXPANDS. Of course, cultivating agriculture began before 1891 and would extend many years beyond 1904. The years 1891–1904 contained critical moments that both made the shift possible and stimulated it. These changes included the introduction of the gasoline engine and electric motor and the formation of the Davis Almond Growers Association in 1897.

The Yolo County Natural Environment. The volatility and harshness of the weather were central problems of both farming and cultivating agriculture. To better convey these problems, this chapter begins with first-person diary accounts by George W. Pierce. We have already met him going back and forth to Davisville. Now he will help us get inside the agriculturalists' world and see the climate problems with which they were coping. In particular, grasping their world helps us understand why they were so receptive to new technology (e.g. gasoline engines) and new forms of organization (producer cooperatives).

8 Feb 1891: Fearful north wind—One of the very worst. Blew chicken yard fence down.

26 July 1891: Very warm. 104 degrees for several hours

1 Aug 1892: Very strong wind this evening—scared us somewhat as it came up suddenly and blew very hard all at once.

30 Nov 1892: Today, one of the hardest rains I ever saw, water fell in torrents and the wind blew a hurricane. The creek raised and . . . water stood in slough six inches above sewer pipe.

[Commenting on 1892 at the end of the year:] A year of earthquakes, high winds, frosts, hot weather out of season, proving a very trying season to both human beings and vegetation.

[Commenting on 1894 at the end of the year:] A disastrous year. Crops were fair. Prices were the lowest ever known. . . . Rains came moderately heavy in early spring. Then stopped for two months and the vegetation suffered. I planted 55 acres to almond trees—they did fairly well only.

5 Jan 1895: Went to Davis. . . . The bridges in this section are all gone . . . The Woodland train is ditched in Hunts field . . . Much fencing is gone. . . Railroad traffic is demoralized.

22 Sept 1895: Last night we nearly had a cyclone—We feared our house would blow away.

[Commenting on 1895 at the end of the year:] This year began by giving us the heaviest flood we have ever had. The creek ran over about two feet deep in our yard. . . Heavy north winds blew our grain out so that the yield was only about half a crop. Prices were very low.

[Commenting on 1896 at the end of the year:] 1896 was a peculiar year. We had a great deal of rain in the spring . . . [But] we had the heaviest frost that we have had in years—a large part of the fruit was destroyed and grain was injured so that the crop was light.

[Commenting on 1897 at the end of the year:] The long continued damp and cold (not frosty) weather was injurious to the fruit and the almond orchard did not set full. April 22 and 23 the north wind blew a gale, fearful on the 22nd, and about one fourth of the almonds were lost—blown off. . . . Grain crops were light.

1 March 1902: Rained and stormed—Blew a hurricane—blew fans out of windmill and blew 190 almond trees down also locust and alantus trees.

Managing the Water Problem: Irrigation. The year-after-year farming conditions depicted by Pierce make it easier to understand that one of the first efforts of agriculturalists would be to devise schemes to control water. For a good part of this period, irrigation efforts were confined to gravity-operated systems. Perhaps the most ambitious of these was for the grapevine orchards of George G. Briggs on the south bank of Putah Creek, near what is now the UCD Mondavi Performing Arts Center. Constructed about 1878, it consisted of "some two hundred miles of concrete pipe . . . laid underground" (7, p. 61). (Remnants of that system are still on the Putah south bank about a hundred yards east of Putah Creek lodge.) In addition, in the 1870s Hugh LaRue developed a system similar to Briggs that stretched from what is now Russell Boulevard to Putah Creek. (The abandoned brick structure just east of the LaRue-Romani home on Russell Boulevard is a remnant of that system.) Other types of systems included windmill-driven water pumps, a scheme with obvious limitations.

The advent of a practical gasoline engine in the early 1890s had a profound effect on the productivity of agriculture in the Central Valley. Beyond pumping water out of the few streams that flowed dependably (which did not include Putah Creek), *well drilling* was now newly attractive because raising water from underground no longer required hand pumping or the windmill. The gasoline engine was joined by the quieter and less noxious electric motor when electrification of the area began after the turn of the century. In this way, technological changes in this period opened the way to agriculture on a scale previously impossible.

Irrigation schemes did not long stay at the level of the individual agriculturist developing a system for a single farm. In 1903 and 1904, the newly formed Consolidated Water Company devised a major Yolo County system of irrigation ditches utilizing water from Clear Lake that arrived in the county via Cache Creek. The May 16, 1903, *Davis Enterprise* opined that "the outlook now is that before the close of another year the irrigation system of Yolo County will be a vast and comprehensive one."

On January 15, 1904, George Pierce made a diary entry on that project. Next to the report he wrote, "Hurrah!" I think we can safely infer he was expressing the sentiments of cultivators countywide.

The activities of the Consolidated Water Company in Yolo County were, of course, only an initial and small step in what would become, within the next fifty or so years in the Central Valley, a colossal scheme for capturing and moving water.

Managing a Marketing Problem: The Davisville Almond Growers Association. Control over water was a major problem on the environmental side, for which irrigation and flood control were solutions. Agriculturists also had major problems on the economic side, for which they devised a social solution.

Not only at the mercy of the weather, they were at the mercy of the market. They pretty much had to accept whatever the market price was at the time they needed to sell a crop. Cultivators of specialty crops like almonds were additionally squeezed by the freight companies, who charged inflated rates for less than a full car load—which an almond grower was apt to have.

What were Davisville growers to do in the face of capricious and/or gouging forces? By 1897, almond growing was widespread among Davisville area farmers-becoming-cultivators. They were likely aware that growers in several other Central Valley locations had, since the late 1880s, formed "dried fruit associations" for the purpose of marketing such products as walnuts as a group rather than as individuals. One of the earliest of these was the Grangers' Business Association, operating at Fresno in 1887. The California Fruit Growers Exchange (subsequently Sunkist Growers, Inc.), established in 1893, is said to have been the first organized farmers' cooperative marketing association (22, p. 7).

The historical record does not reveal the process by which the idea of a producer's cooperative circulated among Davisville almond growers and who had the enterprise and legitimacy to call a meeting for the purpose of forming one. However, we do know that some 15 growers gathered in Davisville on January 23, 1897 to discuss forming an organization. The group appointed a five-person committee to draft a constitution and bylaws and to report on them at the next meeting on January 30.

This second meeting was attended by about 70 people and resulted in forming the Davisville Almond Growers Association. Thirty-one people became initial members, six of whom were elected to an executive committee (which included John Anderson, J.F. Chiles, Jacob LaRue, and George Pierce).

J.O.N., the *Woodland Daily Democrat* "Davisville Doings" columnist, made this report of the event:

> The almond growers of this section have organized and hope, by co-operation, to obtain better prices and more reasonable freights. Heretofore it has been the custom to sell independently, and when the holder offered less than a carload, the buyer took advantage and secured the crop at greatly reduced rates. Now, by combining, full carloads can be secured and the highest prices demanded (*Woodland Daily Democrat*, February 15, 1897).

The association first functioned in the 1897 season. A committee obtained bids and a warehouse. A bid was approved on July 17, 1897, and "the group felt that their initial season had been successful" (22, p. 4).

Pierce and LaRue, among others, believed that a Davisville association alone could not appreciably affect the almond market over the longer term. Larger-scale organization was required. In 1899 and later, they visited almond growers in other locations and were able to convince some of them also to form cooperatives. Gradually, local cooperative associations spread. The efforts eventually led, in May 1910, to a meeting of local associations at which the statewide California Almond Growers Exchange was formed. George Pierce was elected vice-president (8, p. 65).

Almonds should be set in the larger context of other crops in the Davisville/Yolo County area in the late nineteenth and early twentieth centuries. By all accounts, they became *the* leading orchard crop. By the 1930s, the yield would be "nearly twice that of all other fruits and nuts combined" (8, p. 65).

PUBLIC ORDER. The "nuts and bolts" of communities are the institutions and practices that help people organize their relationship to one another. Conversely, some kinds of events, such as fires and large-scale transience, create public order problems. Here are aspects of public order in this period.

William Henry Scott Became the *Davis Enterprise*. As a very young man, Louis A.P. Eichler published the first issue of the *Davis Enterprise* on January 1, 1898. While the venture appeared to go well enough, it was apparently not as attractive as a position with *The California Odd Fellow*, a statewide magazine published in Sacramento. Eichler left to take a job with it after publishing the *Enterprise* for about a year and a half (8, p. 55).

William Henry Scott, a Yolo County native born in 1861, bought the paper from Eichler and assumed the editorship on September 15, 1899. In his first editorial, titled "We Step In," Scott stressed, "No town ever grew without the active aid of the newspaper and vice versa. The paper must have the active assistance of the town, without which failure will be the result" (2, September 22, 1899).

Scott would edit and publish the *Enterprise* "until his retirement in 1935" (Larkey, 7, p. 111). Over these almost 37 years, William Henry Scott *was* the *Davis Enterprise*. In reading the paper year-in and year-out, as I have done, it is clear that Scott wrote pretty much all the stories and reports. The pages of the paper were his personal diary of Davis in a way reminiscent of (but much more elaborate than) George Pierce's diary.

Indeed, Scott's commitment to his paper struck me as beyond making a profit. In fact, I doubt the paper did turn a profit much of the time, but he published it anyway because of his love of Davis. I suspect this because of the assortment of additional bussinesses Scott ran out of the *Enterprise* building. These included his position as the elected Justice of the Peace, an insurance agent, a real estate office, and a job printer. (Although defaced, the *Enterprise* building still stands at 303 G Street. The pictures on pages 72 and 79 show its original charm.)

Slow Growth and the Threat of Non-Davisville Shopping. Davis historian Joann Leach Larkey has characterized "commercial development . . . at the turn of the century" as keeping pace with a "slowly growing resident population and the general prosperity of a diversified agricultural economy" (7, p. 63). As a gauge of the size of Davisville's economy, Larkey enumerated and counted the goods and services advertised in the *Davis Enterprise* in 1898 and 1899. She counted 37 business establishments. This is actually somewhat less than reported by McKinney some 20 years earlier, in 1880 (17, p. 63), as reported in Chapter 2.

On February 1, 1897, J.O.N., writer of "Davisville Doings" in the *Woodland Daily Democrat*, reported that the Sacramento department store Weinstock, Lubin and Company had on a recent Saturday run a chartered, cheap-fare train along the Davis railroad route. Some 700 people were reported to have gotten on it and gone shopping at the "bargain sales" of that store. J.O.N. was alarmed by this practice and wondered if "the department store which today charters a train may in a not very remote future own its own lines . . . and transport patrons free of charge. The department store is a menace to every special dealer and to every small manufacturer in the land."

Saturday, December 9, 1899, this "popular excursion" charter left Davisville at 9 a.m. and the return train left Sacramento at 9:30 p.m. the same day. Although he otherwise decried shopping out of town, editor Scott curiously publicized this excursion on the *Enterprise*'s front page, noting that the schedule "will enable those who desire, to attend one of the popular Saturday evening Band Concerts at the store of Weinstock, Lubin & Co." He even told readers that "a list of the hundreds of special values . . . on this excursion day [is on] the circulars distributed about town" (2, December 8, 1899). (As is said, "Go figure.")

Trains Stopping in Davis. The Southern Pacific Railroad appears to have maintained a rather stable schedule of trains. In May of 1903, for example, the schedule published in the *Enterprise* was said to have gone into effect on January 1, 1901, almost two and a half years before.

However, oddly enough, there were not all that many more than in recent years. In total, 32 trains passed through Davis each day in 1903, 13 of them freight and 19 passenger. Of the 19 passenger, seven went to Sacramento and points north and west and five to San Francisco (meaning Oakland). What is most notably different is that five trains arrived and departed on the north-routed track to and from Oregon and other northern points. Another two, the Oroville passenger, arrived from Sacramento, but did not go on to the Bay Area.

Fire Control and Fighting Problems. Like many another villages, almost all Davisville structures were built of wood. Heating and lighting involved fire in forms that easily got out of control so that buildings burning to the ground were not uncommon. Hotels were particularly dangerous, several of which burned down in the years around the turn of the century. In 1891, the Board of Fire Underwriters set Davisville fire insurance rates high and characterized the village as: " . . . population 700; Fire Fighting Equipment, None; Water Facilities, Not Good" (7, p. 81).

Despite these problems and despite a May 9, 1901, mass meeting to organize a volunteer fire department, there would not be such an organization until after incorporation in March 1917. However, there was one small measure: a derrick-like structure with a metal ring suspended in it was erected at the intersection of Second and G Streets. In the event of fire, one ran to the structure and struck the ring with the hammer provided in order to rouse the citizenry. (The alarm structure is seen in the right-middle of the pictures on pages 69 and 70.)

Troublesome Transients. In this period, rather large numbers of transients gathered at the rail depot and at other locations in Davisville. Editor Scott was especially disturbed by their presence and wrote these, among other, agitated reports:

> [Title:] *More Hobo Thefts*. Every train brings a new delegation of "bos" to town and there are new arrivals by foot every hour of the day. . . . We read every day of the vile acts of these lazy, dirty, low-down scoundrels, so we cannot see how any person can tolerate them. . . . If the ladies would join the crusade by refusing vittles to these worthless scamps it would aid materially in keeping them out of town (2, March 18, 1898).

> [Title:] *The Aggressive Hobo*. The S.P. depot men . . . [say] the hobos [are] . . . so thick about the depot that life to them [is] . . . made burdensome. The lazy critters hover about the transfer tracks like a lot of buzzards and when a transfer man needs a truck he is compelled to brush them aside before he can proceed with his duties. . . . Every morning and evening whole cars [are] filled with the varmints and much . . . valuable time [is] wasted routing them out of the cars, also that they were continually breaking the seals (2, June 20, 1903).

The larger context prompting such transience was the panic in the stock market of 1893 and the economic depression following it. Large numbers of males were economically displaced.

NEW TECHNOLOGY. The last years of the nineteenth century were a period of rapid technological innovation and mass diffusion of those innovations.

Electricity, 1901 and 1903. Private electric lighting of a few Davisville homes apparently preceded lighting public space by two years. In February 1901, the Bay Counties Power Company lighted a private home with a "single globe . . . hanging from a cord in each room." If more than three globes in the home were turned on at once, a device made them flicker as an overload warning (7, p. 73).

A little more than two years later, in June of 1903, the main downtown streets were lit. Judge Scott wrote the following:

> Davisville has after many years of patient-waiting got into the van of electrical progress to the extent of having the electric juice conveyed . . . for the lighting and brightening of the business houses. Nearly all of the business places in the main blocks are wired. However as yet but little has been done toward wiring the dwellings.
>
> *   *   *
>
> It is scarcely to be anticipated that anyone having given them a trial will ever dispense with them. The expense is but very little if any greater than coal oil when everything is considered, to wit costs of lamps, coal oil, breakage, time required to keep them in order . . . to say nothing of the [fire] danger. . . . The board of underwriters have placed a penalty of 25 cents per hundred for each gasoline light used, hence the gasoline is as expensive, with the trouble and danger added (2, June 27, 1903).

The Automobile, 1904. On June 11, 1904, George Pierce purchased the first automobile he had ever owned. It was a Knox, which he bought from a Woodland owner for $900.

It was not only the first auto Pierce had owned; it was apparently also the first one *anyone* in Davis had owned. His diary entries suggest that flat tires, mechanical problems, and excursions began to take up quite a bit of his time. Charmingly, he soon set about to build what he called an "auto house" for it. As a wonderful novelty, he also gave "joy rides" to many people (20, August 24, 1904).

Automobile ownership was not without its social class meaning. On August 24, 1904, Pierce recorded that "Man quit, 'because the boss rides in an automobile while I work for $30.00 a month.'"

The Almond Huller. In 1893, Walter G. Read of Marysville invented and manufactured a machine that removed the hulls from almonds. Naming it the "Sure-Pop," in 1901, he relocated his manufacturing plant to Davisville. He refitted the failed Sinclair windmill plant and was soon employing about 50 people in producing almond hullers that were marketed around the world as well as locally. He died unexpectedly in 1907, and his operation was bought and continued by Theodore G. Schmeiser.

Davis historian Joanne Larkey has characterized the village economy of this period as "lethargic" and noted the excitement that greeted the news of Read's new plant. It was expected to build more than "almond machines" and to be a "general machine shop." This combined with other hopeful signs, editor Scott enthused, "marks the beginning of a new era of prosperity for Davisville and vicinity" (2, December 6, 1900, quoted in 8, p. 56).

Schmeiser Manufacturing. In 1904, locally-born and raised Theodore Schmeiser formed a company to manufacture farm equipment. One of his best known products was the "Good Samaritan" hitch, a device "designed to make every horse in a team pull his share of the load" (8, p. 66). He also invented new farming equipment, including the Portable Automatic Hay Derrick and the Giant Scraper.

CULTURE. Having looked at agriculture, public order, and technology, let us turn to culture.

Boosterism. Richard Orsi defines "boosterism" as the idea "that community goals can be achieved through growth" combined with "an effort to organize the resources of the community to bring about growth, especially through advertising" (*Selling the Golden State*, p. iv). Like people at other California places, Davisville folks appeared to embrace this idea.

Davis's Booster-in-Chief, between 1898 and his retirement in 1935, was William Henry Scott. From virtually the first issue of the *Enterprise* he published to the last, he admonished residents to support the town and to promote its growth. One of his earliest editorials, on February 4, 1898, was a set of booster commandments:

- Never say a word against your town.
- If you spend your cash elsewhere, go elsewhere to get credit.
- Some people never say a good word for their town until they leave it and find there are worse ones.
- United effort will accomplish a great deal. We know a little town of 250 inhabitants, which has a very good water system. That's not Davisville—yet.

The Public Display of Private Life. In Davisville and villages like it, a person's private life seemed to have been public in several respects. If there was a local newspaper, this public display took the form of reporting a resident's participation in social events, visiting in the village, trips outside it, and visitors to the village

The *Davis Enterprise* of 1900 was especially striking in this regard. It had so much zeal along this line that it published *two* such columns. One was on the left side of the front page and titled, "THINGS LOCALLY." It consisted of 20 or so items on the doings of local people. The February 16, 1900 column, for example, began, "Mrs. Petrie is visiting at the home of Otis Wilber." Also: "H.M. LaRue came over from the Sacramento Wednesday morning." "Bert Miller came up from Dixon Saturday evening returning Sunday afternoon."

Apparently some 20 such tidbits were not enough. A second column, titled, "DOINGS IN TOWN by Pauline" appeared on the left side of page three. Pauline, though, was more gossipy and evaluative, as in, "I think Billie and Harry will prefer going to band practice next time," and, "What a blessing it is that Valentine Day only comes once a year, and that is once too often."

In addition, small and private social events were treated as straight news.

MEETING OF THE EUCHRE CLUB
The Euchre Club on last Saturday was entertained by Miss Eta Bullard. Meeting at the home of Miss Bullard instead of G.W. Pierce as formerly intended. Miss Maud Calloway captured the ladies prize and G.W. Pierce the gents. There was a hard battle fought for the latter prize, however, by Dr. Bates and Mr. Pierce, the result being a tie between the two gentlemen which was decided by a cut of the cards, Mr. Pierce being the lucky man (2, February 2, 1900).

Schools. Despite some fluctuation in Davisville's population and a slight upward trend, Joan Larkey reports that

> between 1870 and 1906 the Davisville Grammar School remained fairly constant in staff, student body, and financing. . . . For twelve years between 1889 and 1901, the principal's salary of $90 per month remained unchanged. The 1870 enrollment of 100 pupils increased to 139 in 1887–88, but a picture of the student body in that year shows about one hundred children . . . (7, p. 85).

In June 1902, "it was announced that 77 of 152 Davisville scholars had earned promotion by maintaining grades of 80% or better through out the year" (8, p. 70).

The second of what would be four school buildings in sequence on the block bounded by B-C-Third and Fourth Streets was dedicated in 1903. However, there was a struggle within the school board over supporting bonds to build it. In the board election of June 6, 1902, Mrs. Jakie [*sic*] Grieve, favoring a new school, was faced off against new-school opponent Calvin A. Covell. Grieve won with a margin of 17 among 171 votes cast. She then cast the deciding vote to sell bonds with which to build the school (8, p. 70).

Church Life. On March 25, 1901, the Presbyterian Church of Davisville meeting as "The Session" recorded that it had "51 active members on the roll" and had, therefore, to send "the Presby $8.15, the per capita tax being 16 cents per head" (21, p. 56).

At the Session meeting of June 3 of this same year, 15 individuals or couples were "suspended for inactivity," the illustrious Calvin Covell (and his spouse) among them.

This was no slacker congregation. At this same meeting, congregation members Albert Mastin and Daniel Paterson were each accused of operating a saloon in Davisville. Each was therefore "guilty of immoral conduct in openly owning and running a saloon on the main street of Davisville." June 17 was set as the date for them to appear and answer these charges. Neither man appeared, but the Elder who had delivered the charges reported that both pleaded guilty. "It was then regularly moved, seconded and carried that the names [of each] be stricken from the rolls" (21, p. 58).

The *Minutes* of this period contain other cases of people investigated for or charged with "conduct unbecoming a Christian." Offending actions included "repeatedly been drunk." On May 5, 1905, a person was excommunicated for twice being charged with drunkenness and "failing to reply" to the charge.

Conversely, a number of people were reported as having "presented themselves for examination for membership in the church and were duly accepted into full membership." On November 15, 1903, these included W.H. Scott, who was accepted "by profession."

It is reported that the small Methodist Episcopal church congregation merged with the Presbyterians in the late 1890s (7, p. 106). The village then had only two organized religious groups, the Presbyterians and the Catholics.

The WCTU Forged On. When we left the Davisville WCTU in 1889, it was not doing very well in terms of numbers of members, achieving quorums at meetings, or carrying out program activities. From 1891 to 1904, however, its fortunes brightened somewhat. Reorganized in 1892, persistence paid off and in November the group got permission to place a "wall pocket" containing temperance literature in the train depot. Around this same time, a reading room was opened.

Twelve copies of the state law against the sale of tobacco and liquor to minors were acquired and a decision made to "post them in every place where such was sold" (29, December 17, 1892).

In 1904, there were apparently six saloons in Davis. The prospect of a seventh prompted the group to develop a petition for the purpose of "keeping out the 7th saloon from our midst" (28, March 29, 1904). In a short time, the group had obtained 109 names, but the saloon apparently opened anyway.

Also in 1904, members heard that boys were getting beer at Cloutman's Saloon. An effort to lobby the board of supervisors to close it was not effective. The matter ended in the decision that "all we could do now is to warn Mothers to watch their boys closely . . . " (29, January 7, 1905).

WCTU meetings appeared to be a combination of religious-devotional and social mingling. A meeting began with religious activities such as "prayers were offered for the Saloon Keepers of this place" and "four members . . . offered prayers for the removal of the liquor curse from our midst" (29, November 1 and 8, 1892.) This was followed by an activity such as "a dainty lunch of strawberries and cake with delicious sandwich's and coffee to which we all did ample justice" (29, May 1, 1906).

Festivities. The anti-alcohol sentiments of the Presbyterians and others might prompt one to think that Davisville folks were a reserved and uptight lot. But this seemed not to be the case. The yearly round of life was punctuated by festivities and even revelry.

The kinds of picnics described previously continued. Tammy Grove, however, went out of business when the lodge that sponsored it came onto hard times. It was replaced by the Armstrong Grove of oak and black walnuts located just south of the current Putah Creek Lodge in the UCD arboretum (a grove that is, in part, still there).

The Annual Band Boys Picnic was held there in May 1899 and was written about in the *Enterprise*:

> This is the day of the picnic, and the town has presented a holiday appearance since early morning. Many are here from a distance to enjoy a day's outing. The Grove and dancing platform have been put in excellent shape for the day. The band boys have been practicing for a month and will give some nice music. Games, foot races, bicycle races, a blue rock shoot, baseball game, and the new game of volley ball will take up the attention of those in attendance. Dancing will continue all day and will commence again in the evening.
>
> The baseball game is to be a contest between the Winters and Davisville teams for supremacy and, as both are strong combinations, a good game should result. The blue-rock shoot is under the management of the Peerless Gun Club and will be an interesting feature of the day.
>
> The railroad company has agreed to have the Oregon Express stop at Dixon in the morning so that the Dixonites in attendance can return home on it. It leaves here at 4:35 a.m. (2, May 6, 1899).

Joann Larkey commented on the above report: "Picnics today just aren't what they used to be! But who besides those with pioneer spirit and stamina could stand the pace of such an all-day, all-night picnic and dancing party?" (8, p. 18).

Dances appear to be held with some frequency and there was even an organized dance school and club. Editor Scott reported:

> Davisville holds the banner for its frequent, sociable, jolly dancing parties. Nearly every dance given here has a large attendance. Despite the fact that the dancing school has an average attendance of about thirty couples, the regular club dances every two weeks have from seventy-five to eighty couples present. . . . [At the dance last Saturday] the music was excellent [and] thrilled through the dancers as they glided around the hall. Everyone seemed happy and an evening was never more pleasantly spent (2, February 11, 1898).

Larger-scale and more elaborate dances were called "balls" and attracted participants from other communities. One was the Goose Raffle and another the Grand Ball (8, p. 4). Here is a portrayal of a "Masquerade" ball given on February 2, 1900:

MASQUERADE
A Gorgeous Array of Beauty And Brilliance
THE GRANDEST SOCIAL EVENT OF THE SEASON

For many days the lovers of social sport . . . had been making elaborate preparations. Thursday and Friday a costumer was in town with a choice of assortment of costumes for those not having time or skill to construct their own.

The masters met in the vacant room beneath the hall, and at nine o'clock formed in column of twos and marched up stairs, a motley throng of fanciful and grotesque costumes. The hall was elaborately and tastefully decorated with bunting, Chinese lanterns and flowers.

The floor was in excellent condition. The music was furnished by an orchestra of seven pieces under the direction of Prof. Marvin, and was all that could be desired.

The ball was crowded with maskers of whom there were about one hundred and twenty and many others without masks.

Enjoyment wreathed every face with smiles and filled each heart with gladness. . . . Bucolic swains in Sunday clothes eyed askance the lovely maidens bedecked in all their bewitching array of beautiful textile and color, and hearts throbbed in mutual response as the music smote the chords of love, "and eyes looked love, to eyes that answered back gain," as the young people enfolded in each other's arms, in rhythmic unison glided through the seductive mazes of the giddy dance. It was indeed a scene of gorgeous brilliancy.

At midnight all who felt the necessity for restoring the inner man (and woman) repaired to the Hunt hotel and partook of an elegant supper of which they showed the appreciation done its excellence. Dancing was resumed after supper and the most devout worshippers at the shrine of Terpeicore continued to trip the light fantastic . . ., the final dance taking place about four o'clock, concluding the most enjoyable and successful social event of the season in Davisville.

The ball was given, according to their annual custom, by Golden Seal Lodge, Knights of Pythias, and the members did all in their power to insure its success (2, February 2, 1900).

Editor Scott ended this report with a list of Lodge members who arranged and managed the ball. It was a who's-who of Davisville society, including A.J. Plant, W.J. Montgomery, W.O. Russell, W.H. Scott, and Dr. Bates.

As elsewhere, Davisville people held social events as a way to raise funds. One such was a "lawn party" for the purpose of raising money for the improvement of the cemetery. It took place on August 12, 1903, at the home of Mrs. Granville Cecil. Judge Scott (who also played coronet in the orchestra at this event and performed in a coronet duet) described the scene:

The lawn was . . . lighted with scores of Chinese lanterns hung in rows and in groups. . . . A tent was draped [in the] Stars and Stripes, within the folds of which was the palmist. . . . The guests were continually standing in line waiting their turn and many wended their way homeward disappointedly because of their inability to have their palms read. . . .

The orchestral bower [was] . . . lighted with strong gasoline torches. . . . The parlors . . . were transformed into a veritable tea garden and there the ladies served this popular Japanese beverage in company with stacks of cakes . . . .

Hon. G.W. Pierce . . . admonishing the guests that they expected to have a jolly good time, he then proceeded to announce the numbers of the evening's program, which were . . . [an] overture, by orchestra . . . [performances by] violins, . . . clarinet, cornets, cello, a Recitation, piano solo, . . . vocal solo, . . . Orchestra [two numbers], piano solo . . . concluding with a selection by the orchestra (2, August 15, 1903).

In a era before radio, motion pictures, television, and other externally-manufactured diversions, local people learned entertainment and performing skills and generated their own "hometown entertainment."

There were also the regularly scheduled festivities such as Christmas, Easter, and the Fourth of July. We are fortunate to have a description of the 1898 Sunday School Christmas entertainment held by and in the Presbyterian church. I hope it conveys the distinctive character of religious celebration at the turn of the century.

The cantata and Christmas tree at the Presbyterian Church on Christmas eve . . . was highly appreciated by the large audience assembled. The children executed their parts of the program in admirable manner. . . . The Christmas tree was twenty feet high, reaching from floor to ceiling, bearing 106 twenty-five cent presents—one for each minor pupil in the Sunday School.

Underneath the tree and around its trunk was a pile of 200 sacks containing an apple, orange, nuts, and candy to the weight of one-half pounds each, sufficient in number to supply all Sunday School scholars and all visiting children.

The whole school arranged in four tiers, one above another, in front across the end of the church beside the beautifully decorated forty-candle lit Christmas tree, formed a magnificent picture, long to be remembered by those who saw it (Scott quoted in 8, p. 3).

Chapter Four

RESTARTING DAVIS, 1905–1916

On March 18, 1905, Governor George Pardee signed a bill authorizing the siting and development of a University of California "State Farm." Its main purposes were to be research, education, and public service on agricultural practices suited to California conditions.

A considerable program in agriculture already existed at Berkeley, then the only UC campus. However, agricultural research there was inherently limited by the foggy, damp, cool climate. Most California agricultural conditions were much hotter and harsher. Therefore, a more representative location was needed.

As we have seen, the Davisville area fit this bill. Davisville elites and friendly outsiders had long grasped this fit, and they had begun to organize to get the farm for Davisville, or at least for Yolo County. Unfortunately, people at 76 other locations spread over 13 counties had the same idea (8, p. 90). But Davisville (aka George Washington Pierce) won through.

This winning was a catalytic event that restarted Davisville. Soon, there was an array of new (1) organizations, (2) physical structures, (3) ideas and activities, and (4) problems.

NEW ORGANIZATIONS. There were at least two unsuccessful efforts to site a State Farm before 1905. Yolo County people were aware of this and knew that action would eventually be taken. They had therefore begun to plot strategies well before Pardee signed the bill on March 18. Less than two weeks later—on March 30—a "mass meeting" convened in the Davisville courtrooms (2, April 1, 1905).

A key feature of this meeting was that its participants were an ad hoc gathering rather than an organization. Davisville was a named place, but it had no government aside from the county. Davisville had businesses, but they were not organized as a chamber of commerce or otherwise. These facts are in themselves revealing features of the place on March 30, 1905.

B.B. Tuttle took it upon himself to call the meeting to order, to state its objective, and to request nomination of a chair and secretary. The two well-known (and well-propertied) figures of Jacob Eugene LaRue and Albert Plant were then nominated and elected by the assembled. Discussion ensued and a remarkable amount of progress was made in the task of making Davisville capable of collective, political action. One first and highly facilitating step was taken by Martin V. Sparks early in this meeting. He "pledged his fine farm which adjoins Davisville on the west . . . at a reasonable price" (2, April 1, 1905).

The State Farm Promotion Committee, 1905. The critical matter of available land was thus settled at the start. Attention then turned to forming what the group named the State Farm Promotion Committee (and some called the "Boom" committee). Prominent rancher Sam Montgomery nominated seven people for it. In addition to LaRue and Plant (already elected to run the meeting), George W. Pierce, B.B. Tuttle, G.K. Swingle, O.B. Wilber, and Dr. W.E. Bates were proposed. The assembled elected them, naming George Pierce as the chair. (Pierce's diary entry for this day does not record him as attending this meeting. Instead, he "went to Woodland on State Farm matters.")

A Chamber of Commerce, 1905. At this same meeting, attention turned to "the matter of forming a permanent organization for the town of Davisville . . . " An organizing committee of five was appointed by Chair LaRue. They were Walter Bates (chair), A.J. Tufts, F.P. Smith, A.J. Plant, and former Yolo County supervisor W.O. Russell. This group subsequently met to devise a scheme of organization. In early May, it convened a meeting formally to create the Davisville Chamber of Commerce. Permanent officers were elected and eight committees appointed.

The State Farm Commission began inspecting sites soon after its mid-March creation. It planned to tour six sites proposed in Yolo County on May 20. Arriving by train, the commission began its tour at Davisville. One of the very first tasks of the just-created Chamber of Commerce was, therefore, to meet the commission at the station and to host it.

Indeed, had the Chamber not been created, there would have been no legitimate Davisville group to receive the commission. The pressure to have such a group was especially strong because chambers were the sponsors of most of the 76 competing offers. *Not* to have a Chamber would have been a sign of local lack of interest and/or incompetence. (This Chamber subsequently lapsed, a sign of its narrow purpose and fragile base.)

The Women's Improvement Club, 1905. The Chamber was made up only of men, but apparently felt that women should also help improve the town. It therefore urged women to form their own group, which some of them did on June 16, 1905. They called it the Women's Improvement Club. Its most famous project would be to finance construction of a welcoming arch across G Street at Second. But lack of funds meant that it would not actually be erected for another ten years—in 1916. (The Arch story is told below.)

More immediately, the club held a Grand Ball to raise money to improve the school grounds, which included erecting a fence around it (8, p. 159 and p. 10). The club's activities were intermittent and it was reorganized after inactivity in 1907 and again in 1914 (7, p. 125). At the second reorganization, the Chamber once more asked it "to boost for Davis . . . to aid the Chamber [in every possible way] . . . to aid in beautifying the streets . . ., to secure and maintain proper sanitary conditions, [and] to provide suitable decorations for the town at times when large public gatherings are held" (2, October 24, 1914). Why the Chamber could not do these things itself was not explained

The Business Men's Association, 1916. Perhaps one of reasons the Chamber of Commerce implored others to good works was its own problem of survival. Larkey reports that it had pretty much faded away by 1916. In that year, a new Business Men's Association replaced it. Many of the members of this new group were the same as those in the Chamber of Commerce, but absent the ranchers.

The State Farm, 1906. The most important new organization at or at least near Davisville was, of course, the State Farm. Ann Scheuring has suggested three main reasons it came to be located at Davisville rather than at one of the 76 alternatives. (1) The legislative act did not select a site, as previous failed efforts had done. Instead, the measure enumerated features the site must have. The bill with this approach was initially drafted by Peter J. Shields and State Senator Marshall Diggs from Woodland. The suspicion is that these two men had Yolo County in mind when they drew up the list. Required features included "first-class tillable resources, flexible cropping possibilities, and existing irrigation development" (24, p. 20; 8, p. 95). The irrigation provision was especially important because Davisville met this criteria while a great many others did not (8, p. 35 and p. 93).

(2) The commission's consultant, UC Berkeley Professor Edward Wickson, whom the commission asked for a final recommendation, added location on a major rail line to the list of requirements. This weakened a great many proposals, including that of Woodland, who's site was on a branch line a few miles north of Davis.

(3) Davis had an especially effective committee because it was led by George Washington Pierce. When UCD history professor Richard N. Schwab transcribed Pierce's diaries from the handwritten originals, he also supplied a summary of each year. His overview of Pierce's activities for the period from the signing of the act on March 18, 1905, to the decision for Davisville on April 5, 1906, provides us a close-grained sense of his diligence and skill. A few brief quotes will convey these qualities.

But first, I need to explain the names of the people we will be reading about. The State Farm Selection Commission had five members: Governor Pardee; the Lieutenant Governor A. Anderson; president of the State Agricultural Society B. Rush, who was also a Solano County state senator; UC President Benjamin Wheeler; and State Commissioner of Agriculture E. Cooper. All these men knew politics and had known George Pierce (age 55 in 1905) many years. Pierce and Governor Pardee had attended boarding school together as youth. Elected to the California State Assembly in 1898, Pierce knew first-hand how political decisions were made. The first Central Valley graduate of Berkeley, Pierce attended many UC alumni and other functions and was a longtime acquaintance of President Wheeler. Scheuring observes of Pierce (and of LaRue) that both "were sophisticated people with a variety of social and political connections not only in Yolo County but in the capital" (24, p.16).

Here are Schwab's overviews of Pierce's activities at this time:

> *[1905:]* On the 24th of March Pierce saw Mr. Sparks [local landholder] about locating the Agricultural (State) Farm in

Davisville. (The Davis Campus.) Saw Governor Pardee about it on the 25th. Saw the Governor and the Lieutenant Governor on same matter on the 28th. On the 30th he went to Woodland to discuss the matter. Meeting of committee on the subject at Plant's office on 1 April, discussion at Board of Supervisors in Woodland, 5 April, saw Governor and Lieutenant Governor, 8 April, and had meeting later of State Farm Committee. More intense work, presenting the Davisville site to the State Farm Commission, getting out circulars, April 27th and 28th.

. . . On 17th saw Pres. Wheeler of the University, the Governor, and others about State Farm Commission in Berkeley. More activity on the 19th and 20th of May, with a commission coming on the 20th, including Pres. Wheeler to look at various sites. There are several other entries about this project in this volume of the diary.

On Monday 27th of November Pierce actually offered his own place as the site of the State Farm at a Sacramento meeting of the State Farm Commission!

On 22 December Pierce saw . . . Sparks and got option on his land for State Farm. That was a big step in getting the site for Davis campus. On Sunday Dec 24 Prof. Wickson came up from Berkeley, soil expert, to look at the proposed site for State Farm, showed the Sparks site (20, 1905, p. 1).

[1906:] On Wed 10 Jan. Pierce was still working for the establishment of the State Farm in Davis—mailed maps to Pres. Wheeler and Secretary Henderson on subject, talked with others.

On 10 Feb. Wickson made report to State Farm Commissioners in Sacramento, and all but Davisville, Woodland, Suisun, & Contra Costa sites were eliminated. Working intensely for Davis site in Feb. seeing Gov. Pardee, etc., having meetings. On 16 Feb. got contract for water rights for State Farm. On 19th Feb. collecting subscriptions for State Farm project. On Feb. 26 the Commission visited various sites in Yolo, including Davis. The decision is going to be soon. . . .

The great victory came on Thursday 5 April, 1906 when, as Pierce notes in his diary, the State University Site Commission decided on Davisville at about 4.45 p.m. (20, 1906, p. 1).

The selection of Davisville did not end the matter. The April 5 decision was only a *conditional offer.* Many requirements had to be fulfilled in order to complete the deal. These included providing clear titles to the three pieces of land involved, the actual purchase of all three (the committee only had options), and completing purchase of water rights.

It fell to Pierce to complete these and other tasks. This was all the more difficult because his good friend Jacob LaRue, who lived just down the road at the 2,000-acre Arlington Farm, had died suddenly in January 1906 at age 46. Aside from him, Pierce was the only committee member with the skills to get the job done. He had to go it alone and he did. For want of space, the myriad detailed actions Pierce engaged in from April through October are not reported here. Let me only say that he undertook a great many complicated activities that required much travel and energy in addition to knowledge and political skill.

Let me, though, give my two favorite examples of his work, one of strategic savvy and the other of tenacity. The strategic savvy example involves Martin Sparks. Following Pardee's signing on *March 18, 1905*, Pierce wrote in his diary that, on *March 24*, he "saw Mr. Sparks about locating the Agricultural (State) Farm at Davisville." Now go back to the report of the *March 30* "mass meeting" where the State Farm Promotion Committee was formed. At that meeting, Martin Sparks said he would sell his farm for the State Farm.

This tells us that seven days before the mass meeting, Pierce had approached Sparks with the proposal that he offer to sell his farm for the State Farm. *Pierce had already set up this critical step in the process.* It did not "just happen" nor was it a mere fortunate turn of events. Pierce *constructed* it. (We need also to know that Sparks was 73 years old in 1905 and retired to his family home in Oakland after the sale.)

But this was not the end of Mr. Sparks. Twenty days after Davisville was selected, Sparks wanted to back out and Pierce had to turn him around. Pierce wrote the following in his diary:

> [*April 25, 1906:*] Went to Davisville to see Mr. Sparks who is trying to back out on the State Farm project. Could do but little with him. He finally gave me an option, or said he would give one at old prices provided we would repay him his $500 contribution and pay him interest on this purchase price, $91,250.

The tenacity example involves the San Francisco earthquake of April 18, 1906. That momentous event happened less than two weeks after the decision to put the State Farm at Davisville. But this did not deter Pierce from traveling to Oakland and San Francisco some two weeks later, on May 2 and May 8, to see the U.S. Attorney General and others to nail down titles to the three properties. Of his May 2 trip he observed, "San Francisco's destruction is well nigh complete. It presents a stupendous field of desolation and destruction." He described the May 8 trip as involving a problem in that he was able to walk "down California street to Kearney . . .[but was then] forced to go up to Washington. Climbed debris to Battery, back to Washington and finally to ferry."

This is a report of a 56-year-old man climbing debris in a "field of desolation" for the purpose of clinching a Davisville State Farm deal. *That* is commitment. (Taking all the facts together, I think there is no doubt that Pierce should be regarded as the "father" or founder of UC Davis, rather than others who are sometimes put forth for this honor.)

The first buildings were constructed at the Farm in 1907. The "State Farmers' Institute" on October 29–31, 1907 was its first public event (24, p. 23). Indeed, this event was also the occasion of the formal dedication of the

State Farm itself. The address of welcome was delivered by—who else?—G.W. Pierce. The dedication was attended by more than 500 people (8, p. 86 and p. 142).

Starting in 1908, "Short Courses" for farmers were the first instructional offerings. Resident instruction did not begin until January 1909, when the Farm School opened with 18 enrollees. As described below, the first Picnic Day was also in 1909. The vocational "Farm School" graduated its first class—of nine students—in 1911. The first women university students enrolled for one semester in 1914.

The late 1910s were favorable times for agricultural education in the U.S. American political elites were attempting to upgrade farm life in order to slow the tide of migration to cities. By 1913, the now "University Farm" was headed by a dean rather than a mere superintendent. New buildings included a "third dormitory . . . a beef barn (1914), [and] a classroom and library building (1915)" (24, p. 31). Herds of purebred livestock were started. A Ford Model T was bought for the dean, but he continued to ride a horse—as did President Wheeler at Berkeley (24, p. 31).

Bachelor Girls Book Club, 1909. In the early 1900s, the California State Library established traveling library units. When one was located in Davis, it was called the Davis Free Library and housed in the public school. It was moved to a store and finally to the Buena Vista Hotel (7, p. 113).

On February 21, 1909, the young and unmarried Nettie Marden (later Mrs. Otis Wilber) met with three other young and unmarried women at her ranch home for the purpose of organizing a Bachelor Girls Book Club. According to the *Enterprise* report of this event, the "object of the club is to promote sociability, and to promote the benefit of the Davis Free Library. Systematic effort will be made to secure a permanent home for the library and to have someone in attendance most of the time" (2, February 6, 1909). On April 17, some 20 such "bachelor girls" convened to become the charter members.

The group proceeded to stage a variety of events to raise money for a library building. These included theatrical productions, "library showers," dances, parties, spinning bees, luncheons, refreshments at events, and Picnic Day lunch baskets (7, p. 128; 8, p. 28). How they fared in this quest is described later in this chapter. The rules of membership, however, contained a built-in problem; when a member got married, she had to leave the group. This created instability and reduction in the ranks, leading to reorganization as the Library Club and an early 1930s change in the marriage rule.

NEW STRUCTURES. Along with new organizations, there was an array of new physical structures.

The Davis Arch, 1916. Arches that advertised one's town and welcomed visitors to it were popular civic improvements in the early decades of the twentieth century. They were fairly common in Central Valley towns and a few of them still exist. According to Larkey, the idea of such an arch in Davis grew from the suggestion of a State Farm student. The Woman's Improvement Club adopted the idea as a project (8, p. 10). Davis had no local government to fund such an undertaking, so the $1,280 it would cost had to be raised privately. The club proceeded to hold "endless card parties, bake sales, and benefit entertainments" (8, p. 10).

Also assisted by businessmen contributions and loans, the finished arch was dedicated on October 13, 1916 (2, October 14, 1916). Dedication presider Forest A. Plant recalled an earlier time when "students and townspeople" were not in accord. He declared that "those old days have passed." The arch is a "demonstration of the new spirit of good will—a monument dedicated to the town and UC Farm students alike" (quoted in 7, pp. 124–125).

This is the less interesting part of the Arch's story. The more interesting part is told in the next chapter.

Two Bank Buildings, 1910 and 1913. Curiously, Davis did not have a bank until June 1909, when a Davis branch of the Bank of Yolo opened in a small, wooden building near the northwest corner of Third and G Streets. The next year, a substantial bank building was completed in front of it. (The building is still there, albeit in a run-down condition.) George Pierce was among the otherwise out-of-town investors who brought the bank to town. The June 1 entry in his diary records that he was "the first depositor depositing $500" (20; 8, p. 22).

Some months later, the "temporary quarters" of the Bank of Davis opened in a wooden building a block up the street at the northwest corner of Second and G Streets (pictured on page 73). In 1913, this building was moved across the street and a brick "Prairie School" building replaced it on the same site.

Called the Anderson Building after its owner, J.B. Anderson, it became the commercial center of the town. The ground floor on G Street housed the bank at the corner. Next to it to the north, there was a modern-design post office, one that postal box patrons could access 24 hours a day.

At the ground level along Second Street in the same building, there were three shop spaces. The original tenants were a haberdashery, the Davis Electric Company, and a confectionery and stationary store. "Doctors, dentists and lawyers occupied professional offices in a number of the seventeen rooms on the second floor" (8, p. 148). Joann Larkey reports that the "first concrete sidewalks [in Davis] were constructed in about 1913 as a modernistic addition to the newly constructed Anderson . . . building" (8, p. 8 and p. 148).

A Library Building, 1911. The afternoon of October 3, 1910, "Mrs. Jakie Greive and Mrs. Otis Wilber canvassed the business district" and raised enough money to buy the lot at 117 F Street for the purpose of erecting a library on it (7, p. 113). As reported above, the Bachelor Girls Book Club had begun to raise money for such a facility in 1909. For a cost of $550, the club got a one-room library constructed at 117 F Street in 1911. Furnishings cost another $125. Also in 1911, Miss Harriet Weber was appointed librarian and "continued to serve in this capacity for the next forty years" (7, p. 113).

As a matter of context, we should know that between 1889 and 1923, Andrew Carnegie funded construction of 1,681 library buildings in 1,412 U.S. communities. One hundred and forty-four of these were in California and built between 1899 and 1921. Nearby communities that applied for and received such grants included Dixon (1913), Woodland (1905) and Yolo (1918). But Davis never had such a building and apparently never tried to get one. Why?

Two key conditions were attached to Carnegie library grants. One was that the local community—usually a local government but sometimes a school district—had to promise to fund the new library with a yearly appropriation of at least ten percent of the grant to build the library. The other was that the recipient organization had to provide a suitable site.

Now realize that before March of 1917 Davis did not have a local organization capable of providing a "suitable site" or the ten percent per year funding (except possibly for the school district, which was the recipient in Dixon). When Davis finally became a city in 1917, a different library arrangement had already started. In this way, when the Bachelor Girls acquired 117 F Street and built on it, they foreclosed on the possibility of a Carnegie library in Davis.

Bowers Addition and Acres, 1912 and 1913. In 1912, a newcomer to Davis, a horse-trader and trainer named C.W. Bowers, formed a land development partnership with J.B. Anderson, Del Grieve, and A.M Bracken. It purchased property between what is now Sixth and 11th Streets, and between the tracks and B, for the purpose of residential subdivision. The subdividing was carried out in two phases (8, p. 164).

Started in January 1912, Bowers Addition consisted of the five blocks between G and B and between Sixth and Seventh. Most blocks consisted of 20 lots measuring 50 by 112.5 feet, creating a development total of a little less than 100 home sites. In the *Enterprise* of January 18, editor Scott heralded this plan with the all-caps headline: "GREAT STEP FORWARD FOR A NEW AND LARGER DAVIS." The development was novel in Davis because (among other reasons) the five blocks had cement sidewalks, curbs, crushed rock-covered streets, a tank and pump providing water to each home site, and street trees. Most of the rest of Davis had none of these. Advertisements for the lots invited prospective buyers to "come out" and walk "six continuous blocks of curbing and sidewalk" (11, p. 62, see picture on page 75).

All the lots sold in only a few months. However, homes were built on them at the slow pace of about 25 a decade over the next four decades (11, p. 74). Encouraged by these sales, in mid-1913, Bowers created Bowers Acres on the north of the Addition. While the Addition was built on the idea of a small lot for a residence, each Acre was 100 foot or so east-to-west that ran north and south far enough to be a complete acre (about 400 feet). These 1-acre strips were advertised as home sites for millionaire gentlemen farmers who desired to do some light agriculture. Bowers, indeed, spoke of a millionaire's row developing along the north side of Seventh Street (11, pp. 65-67). But it was not to be. The lots did not sell well and those bought were mostly farmed rather than lived on. Up to the end of World War II, the land north of Seventh remained mostly open country (as seen in the pictures on pages 81 and 82).

New Train Depot, 1913. The original 1868 train depot was jammed rather tightly into the convergence of the tracks headed southwest. Desiring to add new sidings, it was moved some 400 feet northeast in 1901. Then in 1913, the SP built a new "mission-style" depot only a few feet to the east of it. For a time, Davis had two train depot buildings.

Anticipating a new depot as early as 1901, editor Scott opined that year, "The old building has had its day and ought to be retired." Instead, Davis needed a "new and modern structure." (In 1901, the "old building" was 33 years old [2, January 31, 1901; 8, p. 64]).

Having announced a new depot "soon" in 1901, the fact that it did not happen year after year made the topic a running joke. Nevertheless, it was finally built in 1913. Some observers then and now have interpreted it as a supportive SP response to the new State Farm. This, however, seems doubtful. The mission-style building at Davis was one of many such depots SP built in California at that time in order to portray California as an exotic paradise. This and other measures were intended to promote immigration, or least tourism (via riding the train, of course).

The Yolo Basin Causeway, 1916. Ground level travel across the Yolo Basin was often perilous because the area was likely to be under water. Therefore, an elevated road similar to the railroad trestle had to be devised. Begun in 1914 and formally opened in May 1916, this was a mammoth, concrete structure called the Yolo Basin Causeway. In its time, it was considered a construction wonder and billed as the "longest trestle in the world" (8, p. 162). When first built, it was odd or spectacular enough to prompt several postcard producers to market images of it.

A "gala festival held in Sacramento on May 11–14, 1916" heralded its opening (7, p. 38). These multi-day festivities included a May 13 parade—on the structure itself—that was 4.5 miles long and composed of floats from around the valley. The ubiquitous George Pierce, who was one of the conceptualizers and organizers of the festival, wrote in his diary on May 13 that "Davis Philomenian Club took first auto prize. . . ."

The festival highpoint was a mock marriage of the east and west sides of the Central Valley, featuring a wedding party made up of children. Here, Pierce operated even at the detailed level of selecting the children to be the bride and groom. A diary entry for April 27, 1916, reads: " . . . drove to Sacramento to meet prospective bride Miss Bernice Worley, for Causeway Celebration." On May 2, he wrote, "Met all bridesmaids, flower girls, ring-bearer and bride elect at W.L. & Cos for dress fittings and also had photos taken." One May 5, he noted, "Got wands for ceremony."

The causeway's completion stimulated much rejoicing in Davis. It was now very easy to get back and forth between Davis and Sacramento and points east by car.

Subway and State Highway Work. In February 1916, UC gave the state of California a strip of land just to the west of what would become the site of the Boy Scout Cabin. The site was to be used for a railroad underpass or "subway," a structure subsequently named Richards Underpass.

This was part of the larger project of constructing a state highway from Sacramento through Davis. In this same period, the state was still acquiring rights of way between these two places. One of these involved condemnation of property south of the tracks "to permit a favorable approach to the subway" (2, January 15, 1916). There were delays and the actual construction of the subway did not begin until 1917.

NEW CULTURE. What we might think of as the "real stuff" of social life is not organizational or physical structure. Instead it is people's ideas about what is true, moral, and valuable.

A New Name, 1906. When people undergo dramatic changes of personal identity, they sometimes change their names. Something of that sort happened in Davisville in 1906. The Saturday, April 7, 1906, issue of Scott's newspaper was called the *Davisvillle Enterprise*. But the next issue, Saturday, April 14, 1906, was the *Davis Enterprise*.

Recall that Davisville was announced as the site of the State Farm on Friday, April 6. Over the week between the announcement and the next issue of the paper, Scott decided the change. Of it, he wrote in the April 14, 1906, issue, "the 'ville' attached signifies a countryside place of insignificant import, and we believe it . . . should be eliminated . . . " (2). Subsequently, Scott, with others, petitioned the U.S. post office for this same change. Twenty months later, on November 7, 1907, the request was granted (49 years after the founding of Davisville).

Picnic Day, 1909. In May 1908, George Pierce and several friends gathered for a picnic at the State Farm, an event that was also a celebration of the farm itself. Some observers say this gathering was the model for the first official Picnic Day the following year (8, p. 120). Held on May 20, 1909, it was conceived as an "open house" to which the public was invited to inspect the work of the farm while having an enjoyable outing. One major event that day was the dedication and opening of North Hall, the first dormitory. "Advertised statewide, the event drew an estimated 3,000 people . . . to see the University Farm on full display" (24, p. 36). George Pierce and his family attended. His May 20 entry reads:

> Decorated auto with blue and gold trimmings. All went to State Farm picnic taking Mr. Troutman . . . who played baritone in band. Was on program for an address on "the education of the Farm Boy." There was a very large attendance estimated as near 2000 people. Winters came in 20 or more automobiles.

Over the years, this event would become ever larger and a significant occasion for all of Davis, not just the State Farm. By 1916, with the Causeway available, some 15,000 people attended. Governor Johnson and UC President Wheeler were speakers, indicators of a significance not accorded it for many decades afterwards (20, April 22, 1916).

Lincoln Highway Frustration. In 1913, an automobile manufacturing group met in Detroit to form the Lincoln Highway Association. Its purpose was to promote hard surface highways. One way to do this, the association thought, was to lay out a cross-country auto route between New York and San Francisco. Only a very small number of that 3,500 miles was paved. So, they had their work cut out for them. Notice that this was—in highway jargon—a "private road." For this reason and despite pestering him about it, Henry Ford refused to support the plan because he thought roads should be publicly funded. Note also that the association was not building roads; it only conducted campaigns to have others do it.

Before the exact route was selected, the association announced it was going to publish a map and a manual intended to encourage people to embark on cross-country motor trips, something that was at this time rarely done and very arduous. After publication, the manual and route would be revised from time to time.

The prospect of such a motor route created competition among communities anywhere near where it might run. Editor Scott got on this bandwagon right away and was among Davis leaders who lobbied the California Lincoln Highway people to run the route through Davis. To great disappointment, the first route came to Sacramento but turned south to Stockton, and then west through Livermore and into the ferry terminals at Oakland. Indeed, the route selected disappointed many towns across the nation, but the association stuck with the principles of the least obstructed, most direct course.

In the case of Davis, the rationale was that, before 1916, it was too difficult to cross the Yolo Basin. After 1916, the rationale for not changing the route was the lack of a bridge at the Carquinez Strait and the poor ferry service there. When the Carquinez Bridge opened in mid-1927, the route to Davis was added as an "alternative." However, even this smaller glory was short-lived. By this time, the federal government had begun to finance road building and decreed that roads it financed would be numbered rather than named. Seeing the handwriting on the wall, the Lincoln Highway Association disbanded on the last day of 1927. With this, the highway ceased to exist. So, it can be said that Davis was on the Lincoln Highway for about six months in 1927.

Liquor Suppressed, 1911. Now that the State Farm was located at Davis, prohibitionists set about to end-run local voters who had already twice voted (in 1874 and 1907) not to close the saloons (7, p. 119). Turning to the state legislature, George Pierce lobbied for a state law banning saloons as a way to protect college students at Davis. As we have seen, Pierce had served as a member of the California State Assembly and he therefore knew the mechanics and politics of law-making. His journal records such actions as, "Had Judge Shields draw bill for liquor suppression" (20, January 27, 1909). Interestingly, several members of the legislature he approached declined to introduce the bill. However, on February 11, 1909, Pierce wrote, "Finally got no-saloon bill fathered by Senator Black of Santa Clara." In March 1911, it passed both houses "like greased lightening," in the words of editor Scott (2, March 11, 1911).

It had then to be signed by Governor Hiram Johnson. At the request of what the *Sacramento Union* called "the saloon men of Davis," the governor granted a special appeal hearing before him later that March. Representatives of both sides appeared. The pro-salooners argued that closing would hurt the local economy and that students did not frequent the saloons anyway. Jakie Grieve, owner of the Buena Vista hotel (which had a bar), pointed out the irony that the saloon owners had vigorously contributed both time and money to getting the State Farm, only now to be betrayed. She declared that the "residents would rather have the saloons than the Farm if the choice had to be made between the two" (2, quoted in 8, p. 153). Anti-saloon claims included the assertion by a University Farm administrator that saloons were "having a deterrent effect upon the attendance, and that one boy had been expelled for drunkenness . . ." (8, p. 151). The governor decided in favor of liquor suppression. This was the law in Davis until the legislature lifted the ban starting on January 1, 1979. (George Pierce's desire to protect students from liquor and his own teetotalism did not stop him from entering in his diary on August 20, 1928, "Went again [into Davis] in p.m. for a pint of liquor for medicinal purposes.")

PROBLEMS. A number of matters are not easily characterized as organization, structure, or culture. They are, instead, problems.

Big Fires. Recall that in the previous period, fires were recognized as a major problem, but this did not lead to an effective plan for dealing with them. This state of affairs continued throughout this period. However, fires were not constant. They got larger. Three of the largest took place in 1906, 1909, and 1916. Scott said of the 1906 fire that while is was appalling, "it was nonetheless a grand pyrotechnic display" when it consumed the Read plant's 70 foot water tower, whose water was not used to fight the fire (2, June 2, 1906).

Pierce described the major fire of August 20, 1909, as burning from the " 'old' corner Dietrich's to the Hoffman house, burning the old Hunt livery stable, Silvas's dwelling, the hardware storeroom, a pino house, the bank, a vacant store room and A.J. Tuft's storeroom and poultry shed. . . . "

The fire of November 12, 1916, was the largest of the period and burned down more than half of the west side of G Street in the main business block. Pierce wrote that on a trip to Davis he "found that all the west side of [then] Olive Street from Hoags store to Odd Fellows Hall had burned since 11 a.m. Two fire engines from Sacramento and a fire train from the S.P . . . came to assistance. . . ." (20, November 12, 1916).

An Unsanitary Town. On December 8, 1914, state of California sanitary inspector Edward Ross made an unannounced visit to Davis for the purpose of assessing its water, sewage, and garbage systems. Dated January 11, 1915, a copy of his report was sent to Justice of the Peace Scott and Dr. Bates as the "Health Officer." Editor Scott summarized the findings in the *Enterprise* of January 16, 1915, conveying that the board thought that Davis had serious problems with its water, sewage, and garbage. And while the state would be reasonable, Scott went on, this is "no child's play proposition . . . [The board's] suggestions must be complied with and [the inspector] will return later to observe progress" (2).

I tracked down the report in the California State Archives and found these main conclusions:

> No sewer system is provided. . . . [The] vault privies . . . [are] in many instances in dilapidated and filthy condition, especially in the business section . . .
>
> Water. . . wells . . . are in many instances . . . within fifty feet of vault privies or cesspools . . . . There is no . . . system for the removal of garbage. . . . Manure, etc. are allowed to accumulate for months and even years . . .
>
> The streets are . . . in bad condition allowing the water, etc. to collect and form stagnant pools. . . . Hog pens are located about sixty feet and the cow barns about two hundred feet from the [Buena Vista] hotel. The manure . . . is allowed to collect in the barn yard for months. . . .

The report concluded with a detailed set of recommendations for remedying these problems.

*   *   *

In this chapter we have seen the people of Davis begin to cooperate on public projects. Most dramatically, they were able to work together as the State Farm Promotion Committee, the chamber of commerce, and the Bachelor Girls.

However, we have also seen that civic action was fragile. A vote to incorporate as a city failed in 1911. Efforts to form a true fire department were unsuccessful (8, p. 117). Several important organizations founded in this period did not survive very long. There was still no local government. Water, sewage, and garbage posed serious health dangers, but there was little public action.

Chapter Five

URBANIZING DAVIS, 1917–1929

The period 1917–1929 was a "golden age" for Davis. In it, the technical systems that make city life possible were installed and many of its now-historic buildings were constructed. It became less of a primitive village that lacked amenities (even a government) and started to become more urban.

Even so, Davis had major problems. These included the inability to fight fires, provide adequate water, dispose of sewage, to stop street-generated dust storms, and backwardness in the eyes of University Farm students.

The story of this golden age is organized in terms of new organizations, physical structures, and culture.

NEW ORGANIZATIONS. To urbanize a place is (among other things) to increase organized efforts to keep public order and to provide education.

Incorporation: The City of Davis, 1917. After a vote to form a city failed in 1911, the three serious fires described in the previous chapter fanned new sentiments favorable to incorporation. The third of these fires, on November 12, 1916, which burnt half the main business block, was apparently the last straw. Eight days later, the Davis Business Men's Association convened a "mass meeting" to focus on fire protection and water supply. At this meeting, someone literally put a petition on a table that was addressed to the Board of Supervisors and requested an incorporation election. Forty-six people signed it. A minimum of 60 was required for Board approval. The minimum was exceeded in subsequent days (8, p. 57). Presented to the Board on January 27, 1917, March 20 was set as Election Day. This time, the proposition triumphed at the polls with a vote of 317 to 87.

Civil Order Created, 1917–1918. To institute a government is to begin a new order of living. It is interesting to inspect the laws the trustees thought important to adopt as the first matters of business in this new order.

Of the first 17 ordinances promulgated in 1917–1918, nine called a civil order into existence. In the sequence of their adoption, these were: business licenses; firefighting; explosives control; building regulations; obstructions of sidewalks declared a nuisance; a board of health established; proper use of streets and other public ways specified; banning of roaming livestock, dry weeds, and running dogs; and a requirement to wear a gauze mask in public (to protect against influenza, which was a serious danger at the time).

The other eight ordinances established a regular time to meet, a police force, duties of government officers, two kinds of taxes, a city attorney, elections, and an elaborate code of misdemeanors.

It is notable that this first government did not immediately engage in public works, such as paving streets or installing a water or sewer system (none of which Davis had), or initiate amenities, such as parks. By unanimous votes, the founding government concentrated, instead, on pubic safety and especially on civil order.

Trustee Administrators. As a government with no staff to speak of, members of the new Board of Trustees assumed the responsibilities of administering city functions. The first formulation of these functions were: fire and police; streets, sidewalks and parks; light and power; and health and safety. This system of direct administration by Board (later Council) members continued for many years.

In reading accounts of how this worked, the level of competence and command of detail called for by these administrative roles was impressive. In contrast, contemporary Council members need no command of detail and administrative skill *at all* (and sometimes show breathtaking ignorance and incompetence). This is because city government now has large and specialized staff. In this way, these early elected officials mastered more demanding circumstances and required more organizational competence than current office-holders.

Organized Firefighters, 1917. As one would expect, the Trustees quickly organized a firefighting force by naming a chief of firefighting and a 15-man volunteer corps. The chief was Walter Lilliard. He met with his force once a month at his business, which was Lilliard's Grocery Store at Third and G (7, p. 81). The first fire truck was acquired in 1918, a Studebaker "carrying a fifty-five gallon soda-acid chemical tank and two hundred feet of hose" (7, p. 81).

War Organizations, 1917–1918. World War I—The Great War—was declared on April 6, 1917, and victory proclaimed on November 11, 1918. This period of almost two years caused many important—albeit temporary—changes in everyday life in Davis. Its intrusiveness into ordinary activities was on a scale that would not be seen again until World War II.

This intrusiveness went down to the level of organized regulation of food. By March 2, 1918, the State Council of Defense decreed that "only two ounces of 'Liberty bread' (a government-approved, grain-saving formulation) would be served to customers in eating houses" (2, March 2, 1918, quoted in 8, p. 33). This organization also urged home gardens as a form of patriotic service. Public schools were enlisted in the food effort in the form of Freedom Gardens on school grounds, one of which was cultivated behind the school on Third Street between C and B Streets (pictured on page 78).

The Northern Branch of the College of Agriculture. World War I caused State Farm enrollment to drop from 314 to 75. But it sharply rose to almost 600 in 1919. Crowded students lived in temporary tents and an appeal was made to townspeople for rooms (24, p. 49). In 1922, the farm's name was changed to the Northern Branch of the College of Agriculture and the faculty was nearly doubled. Beginning that same year, students were allowed to earn a four-year degree at Davis without doing the first two years at Berkeley.

New buildings of this period were substantial and included: *1921*, a recreational gym; *1922*, Horticulture Hall, Dairy Industry (later Roadhouse) Hall; *1927*, Agricultural Engineering (later Walker) Hall; and *1928*, Animal Science (later Hart) Hall. The main campus roads were paved in 1928.

In 1922, the original Farm School curriculum was discontinued and replaced by a "non-degree" curriculum. Entrance remained easy, but the courses of study were reorganized into programs leading to certificates of completion. This curriculum "emphasized the practical rather than the academic [and was] particularly popular with foreign students and those who expected to return to family farming operations" (24, p. 49).

These improvements in the "Branch" were the outcome of complaints, the pressure of group lobbying, and perception of threats to the future of the campus and the town. A farmer lobby group organized in 1919—the Agricultural Legislative Committee—considered conditions at the University Farm after the war "almost a scandal." It demanded major upgrading, which resulted in the state government creating a Special Legislative Commission on Agricultural Education. The recommendations of this commission, combined with other brouhaha, led to the major changes indicated above and to many others (24, Chs. 2 and 3; 8, p. 124).

In addition, some Davis residents were disquieted by the idea that the farm was not up to par. Indeed, the son of the first Davis mayor was, in 1920, reported to have decided to enroll in the agricultural college at Oregon State rather than at Davis. This "despite the fact that his home . . . is just across the highway from the Farm School," editor Scott wrote. Worse still, some 200 agricultural students were said already to be enrolled in Agriculture at Oregon State (2, September 10, 1920; 8, p.122).

This student defection prompted the question, "What *does* Davis have to offer the university student?" Civic leaders such as Lynn N. Irwin were prepared to say "not much" and a new Community Services club geared to reform was organized and elected officers in November 1920 (8, p. 122).

High School District Formed, 1925. The rapid growth of the Branch Agricultural College created enrollment pressure in the local schools. In particular, it created a high school access problem. Historically, Davis children attended high school in Woodland. By 1923, this involved weekday transport of 50 to 60 students to Woodland and back. Davis people started to think about forming their own high school. This was strongly opposed by the Woodland district, which argued it was much cheaper for Davis formally to join Woodland.

Professor C.L. Roadhouse argued that if Davis joined Woodland it would be difficult ever to form a Davis high school. Therefore, people in Davis needed to forge ahead. He spearheaded a committee with the purpose of purchasing a high school site. Thirty-nine people met in May 1923 to consider purchasing the for-sale block bounded by B, C, Fifth, and Sixth Streets.

Thirty-four of those present pledged $100 each and two pledged $50 each. The block was bought (8, p. 111). This would not, however, be where the high school was built, nor did it immediately lead to a high school.

Instead, what Larkey terms "legal technicalities" threatened and stalled the project. Undeterred, the trustees of the Davis grammar school decided, as a stop-gap, to organize the first year of a high school in a new wing of their school. A bond election for this purpose was held in June 1924 and adopted by a vote of 178 to 14.

Meanwhile, a campaign to form a high school district was underway. Formation required a majority vote of voters in each of the four districts that would make it up: Plainfield, Davis, Montgomery, and Fairfield. In the initial election, the Plainfield outcome was challenged and the Yolo County Superintendent of Schools, Miss Harriett Stoddard (the founder of Mothers Day, by the way), refused to certify the results. But all was not lost. The Plainfield district was subsequently dissolved for want of enrollment. On June 1, 1925, the new high school district was formed from the remaining three. (The five trustees elected included a man with whom the reader is now well familiar: George Pierce [8, p.110]).

The organizational way was now clear, but money had to be raised for the building itself. I pick up that part of the story in the section on the high school building later in this chapter.

Space constraints allow no more than listing the founding of quite a number of other important organizations: *1920*, Boy Scouts of America; *1921*, garbage collection begins; *1922*, Cemetery District incorporated; *1925*, Chamber of Commerce, Planning Commission and Zoning Ordinance; *1926*, Davis Rotary Club; *1927*, traffic officer/chief of police appointed; 1928, change to mayor-council system.

The organizations described or listed in this chapter are notable for the relative lack of those that are "economic," entities that manufacture, distribute, or retail products. Davis certainly had perhaps a hundred or so entities in the retailing category. Manufacturing and distributing organizations were a different story. As far as I can tell, there were few of either of these. Instead, its major "manufacturer" was the University Farm/Agricultural Branch College/College of Agriculture at Davis.

NEW STRUCTURES. Relative to previous periods, 1917–1929 was a time of much new construction. (However, relative to other places—such as Woodland—these structures were not very numerous, large, or architecturally impressive, but that is another matter.)

Subway Completed, 1917. Soon after it opened in the last days of 1917, editor Scott raised the question of whether it was any safer than the old at-grade crossing. Proceeding west along Olive, the road required a sharp right into the subway followed by a sharp left onto First. Neither of these turns were signaled by signs and there was no lighting at night (2, January 12, 1918). Scott's concerns would prove to be valid. The subway was the site of numerous and serious accidents for many years (8, p. 156).

Open Sewage Versus a Municipal Water System, 1919. Recall that a state board of health inspector visited Davis in December 1914 and did not like what he found. A board inspector made a second visit on September 27,

1919, which resulted in an even more negative assessment. Among alarming conditions was sewage floating on the surface of empty lots near the University House hotel at Second and B. According to the report, the limit on the number of cesspools had been reached, but the discharge was ever increasing.

At this time, Mrs. C. Schmeiser operated the hotel and she wrote to the board requesting an exception to the cesspool limit. The director of sanitary engineering (Mr. Gillespie) responded in the negative. He then went on to remark about Davis in general:

> Conditions at Davis are as serious as any this board has run across. I am really surprised that an enterprising town, favored moreover by the presence of a great educational institution, should be so backward. . . . Your people do not appreciate the hazards . . . when it allows sewage to spread about on the surface of the town lots [as was the case at Second and B]. (2, November 17, 1919).

Mr. Gillespie wrote further that while the board could not compel building a sewage system, it could (and would) shut down unsanitary conditions. If it did that, both of the Davis hotels and many other establishments "would have to go out of business."

The conditions highlighted in the first report of January 1915 (described in the previous chapter) were still there, but now had this new surface pools-of-sewage wrinkle. Davis was becoming a victim of its own successful growth and new construction. New and larger buildings such as University House and the Anderson Building were well patronized, but served only by septic tanks that overflowed into cesspools, which themselves overflowed or were pumped out onto adjacent open ground when full. The Anderson Building at Second and G also had several cesspools in adjacent lots, but these were insufficient. The report of the second inspection says that "sewage is dumped directly on the ground and the next door neighbor claimed that the odor at such a time was so bad that she was literally compelled to leave home for a day or two" (2, October 17, 1919).

This overflow problem was not confined to larger buildings downtown. Residents had the same problem. According to the chair of the first planning commission, "everyone was on cesspools and when we had a wet winter, which meant twenty inches or over, the cesspools would fill up and raw sewage would flood the backyards" (8, p.136).

The rub in all this is that the town badly needed *both* a sewage and a water system. However, it could only bond up to a legally-limited portion of the valuation of its structures. That limit meant that it could only afford to build a sewage *or* a water system in 1919.

Amidst much debate, the trustees voted to issue a bond for the water but not a sewage system. A city election on the $75,000 in bonds needed was held on November 4, 1919, and it passed by a three to one ratio (2, November 7, 1919).

Sewer System, 1921. The long-postponed and chronic sewage problem was finally acted on in January 1921. A bond issue for it was approved by a vote of sixteen to one.

This unusually consensual civic action came in the context (mentioned above) of a University Farm that was under attack as an inferior place that students would not attend. Instead, dozens if not hundreds were studying agriculture at Oregon State in preference to Davis because the campus *and the town* were seen as backward. Such student perceptions radically threatened the future of Davis itself and not merely the Farm. It was for such reasons that editor Scott penned this among other such headlines: "Give Us Sewers and All Will Be Fine." After the election he rejoiced, "Davis Now Takes Her Place in the Forum" (8, p. 122). Work on the sewer system began in March 1921 and residents were required to connect to it by January 1922 (7, p. 72).

College Park Subdivision, 1923. In local sentiment, housing in Davis locales such as Bowers Addition was not adequate for University Farm faculty. Joann Larkey wrote in 1972 that "from all reports . . . [early] homes in the Bowers Addition left much to be desired in the way of convenience and aesthetic qualities, although they are all still occupied today" (8, p.130). More upscale, dignified, and stately homes were wanted, especially for faculty recruitment.

College Park was born of such social class striving. In the spring of 1923, a five-man group formed a plan for a 25-acre new subdivision a quarter of a mile west of the Davis city limits. The plan was organized as a non-profit corporation in which "anyone" could buy a lot. A public meeting inviting participation was held in June 1923 and "25 men . . . signed up for lots" (8, p. 141). The corporation then formed provided restrictions in order to make it "as near an ideal residence section as possible." In addition to the usual rules on such things as setbacks and commercial use, as in the Bowers Addition earlier, participants pledged that no one would live there "other than those of the Caucasian race" (8, p. 141).

Established *outside* the city limits apparently without objection from city officials, College Park thus became Davis's first (but far from the last) major leapfrog and tax-avoiding development.

Street-Paving, 1923 and 1924. The streets of Davis were eventually paved. But this did not happen without considerable cajoling by editor Scott in the pages of the *Enterprise*. On March 2, 1923, for example, he tried to shame residents with the story that Suisun had recently had a volunteer day on which residents hauled loads of gravel to cover many of its streets.

> Why could not the same program be carried out in Davis? We all know the streets are in rotten condition. When a wind comes up it looks like we were in the Sahara desert. Dust, dust and then MORE dust. . . . With voluntary labor . . . at least some of the streets could be rounded into shape so that we would not have to eat coupla [*sic*] pounds of dirt every time we face a wind (2, March 2, 1923).

Continued on page 101

Decade	Decade-start Population (in thousands)/ square miles	Period	Years	Number of Years	Key Features
1860s	0.0/0.0	**Before Davisville/Davis**			
		1. Expectant	1868-71	4	People expectantly rush to a new future.
1870s	0.5/0.4	2. Farming	1872-90	19	Population and construction plateau. Dry crops, grain shipping, and farm machinery key in the local economy.
1880s	0.4/0.4				
1890s	0.5/0.4	3. Cultivating	1891-1904	14	Plateau continued. Cultivated and irrigated agriculture expand, particularly almonds.
1900s	0.7/0.4	4. Restarting	1905-16	12	A successful campaign to be the site of the University of California Experimental Farm rejuvenated the stagnant village.
1910s	0.8/0.4				
1920s	1.0/0.4	5. Urbanizing	1917-29	13	Responding to state government prodding, urban amenities were installed, including a water and sewage system. Zoning and a General Plan were adopted.
1930s	1.2/0.4	6. Depression	1930-45	16	The worldwide economic depression hit Davis. Ironically, New Deal programs financed local improvements, including curbs and the first City park. Local politics continued to be highly consensual/clique dominated.
1940s	1.7/0.4				
1950s	3.6/1.1	7. Exploding	1946-71	26	Like many other places in California, Davis exploded in population and construction after WWII. The now UC Davis general campus was a major generator of growth. Unlike other cities, Davis leaders resisted large peripheral shopping centers and adopted polices to make a "core area" the city-center.
1960s	8.9/2.0				
1970s	23.5/6.2	8. Progressive	1972-89	18	Unsettled by growth, in the City Council election of 1972, voters favored what would be the first of a series a "progressive" Councils that implemented slower growth and environmentally informed policies. Davis developed a national image as environmentally forefront.
1980s	36.6/6.9				
1990s	46.3/8.6	9. Contested	1990—	15+	"Moderate" versus "progressive" political tendencies crystallized with protracted struggle over the rate and character of growth.
2000s	60.3/9.9				

I. 1. *Nine Periods of Davis History.* *This chart provides an overview of nine periods of Davis history, which are also the nine numbered chapters of this book.*

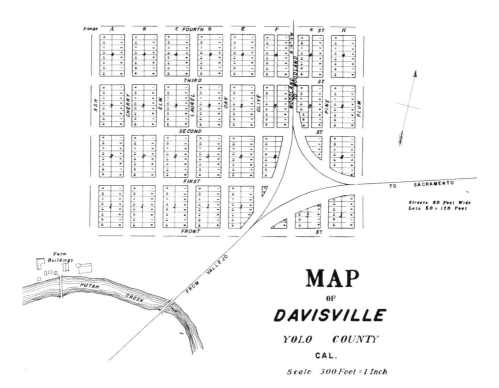

1. 1. The 1868 Davis Street Grid. *As initially conceived, the town was a four-by-eight rectangle of 32 blocks. This grid has remained essentially intact. As seen here, the north-south streets were at first named for trees. (UC Davis Special Collections.)*

1. 2. Looking North up G from Second Street, 1870. *This is apparently the first of what would become thousands of views "looking north up G Street" taken over subsequent decades. A number of these are reproduced in this book and in* Davis, California: 1910s–1940s *(15). (UC Davis Special Collections.)*

2. 1. First General Merchandise Store, Southwest Corner First and G Streets, 1875. *The gentleman labeled "Pierce" is George Washington Pierce, father of the same-named Pierce subsequently a key figure in Davis history. In this year, the younger Pierce is a senior at the University of California in Berkeley. (UC Davis Special Collections.)*

2. 2. Archetypal Mule-team and Harvester. *This is one of thousands of nineteenth-century photographs of mule teams pulling harvesters. These men-mule-machine ensembles drew attention because they were spectacular. Several operating in an area at the same time "literally marched across wheat fields like an army" (24, p. 6). (Hattie Weber Museum.)*

2. 3. Loaded Wagons Lined up at a Davisville Warehouse, c. 1900. *Prior to the railroad, such wagons had to make their way to boats at Knights Landing or Suisun. (Hattie Weber Museum.)*

2. 4. Scale and Scale-house at Fifth and G, c. 1907. *A wagon loaded with grain stopped on the scale, to the left, was weighed, and moved on. (UC Davis Special Collections.)*

2. 5. *Grain Storage Warehouses*, c. *1905*. *Grain warehouses lined the tracks north of Third (crossing in the middle ground). (Hattie Weber Museum.)*

3. 1. G *Street Looking North from First Street*, 1895. *The fire alarm tower at Second and G is seen in the middle-right. The Lillard Hotel (built 1884, burned down 1898) is on the left. The sign on the front of it reads "SALOON." (Larkey Collection.)*

3. 2. G Street Looking North from Second Street, c. 1907. *The intersection of Second and G is on the left, with the fire alarm tower on the right. An early almond huller is in the foreground. (Larkey Collection.)*

3. 3. Wagon Loaded with Bags of Almonds, c. 1900. *Leaving the George Pierce ranch bound for Davisville, this load will be stored and marketed cooperatively by the Davisville Almond Growers Association. (Pierce Collection, UC Davis Special Collections.)*

3. 4. George Weber Saloon, Second and G, 1890. *Mr. Weber is pictured sixth from the left. The man standing apart on the far right was called "China Joe." The social meaning of the physical distance between the six men on the left and China Joe has been the subject of much comment. (Hattie Weber Museum.)*

3. 5. George Weber Family and Mansion, Northeast Corner, Second and G Streets, c. 1900. *From the left: Ida Weber Grieve (daughter), a visitor, Hattie Weber (daughter), Annie Weber Montgomery (daughter), Ann Weber (wife), Georgens Montgomery (granddaughter), Gertrude Weber (daughter, later Mrs. Sam Brinley). (Hattie Weber Museum.)*

4. 1. *Davis Structures in 1905.* *In this year, the village contained 177 buildings. (Excerpt from U.S. Geological Survey, California Swingle Quadrangle, 1905.)*

4. 2. G Street (then called Olive) Looking South, c. 1910. *White with an oval window, the Bank of Yolo is on the right and at the northeast corner of Third and "Olive." (UC Davis Special Collections.)*

4. 3. Temporary Quarters, Bank of Davis, 1912. *Constructed at the northwest corner of Second and G, this building was moved and replaced by the Anderson Building (shown in picture 4.4) in 1914. (Hattie Weber Museum.)*

4. 4. Looking North up G Street, c. 1915. *The new Anderson Building is on the left. Informally, Davisites called Olive/G Street, "main street," as the photographer has done here. (David Herbst.)*

4. 5. *The Mission-style Depot shortly after Construction, 1913.* The Southern Pacific Railroad replaced many of its Victorian-style stations with this "mission" style as part of a larger effort to promote California immigration and tourism. (David Herbst.)

4. 6. *The Davis Arch, 1916–1924.* This symbol of town-gown solidarity was built with private funds raised by the Women's Improvement Club and other groups before Davis was an incorporated place. Considered an impediment to rapidly increasing automobile traffic, it was taken down in 1924. (Irl Rickabaugh.)

One shipment of a train load of READ SURE POP ALMOND HULLERS & SEPARATORS shipped July 30th, 1912, by the Schmeiser Manufacturing Co., Davis, Calif.

SEE US AT THE STAT FAIR AT SACRAMETO, CAL. SEPT. 14 to 21-1912.

4. 7. Almond Hullers Postcard, 1912. *Schmeiser Manufacturing produced innovative farm machinery at its buildings in the vicinity of Second and I Streets. These included almond hullers, shown here loaded for shipping. (David Herbst.)*

4. 8. Advertisement for Bowers Addition, Davis Enterprise, *Friday March 13, 1913. *The phrase "come out" suggests a significant distance, although Sixth and G was only four blocks north of Second and G, the center of town.*

Have You Seen The Improvements

IN THE

BOWERS ADDITION

Come out tomorrow and see the sidewalks, curb & street work
Six continuous blocks of curbing and sidewalk completed
LOTS 50 X 112½ TO AN ALLEY and FACING 80 FOOT
STREETS ONLY $250.
ALL IMPROVEMENTS FREE TO LOT BUYERS

MT. DIABLO REALTY CO.

Enterprise Building   Davis, California

4. 9. The Women's Improvement Club, c. 1915. *Too numerous individually to identify, this picture includes many of the most prominent Davis women of this period, including Mrs. George Pierce and Miss Hattie Weber. (Hattie Weber Museum.)*

4. 10. Crowd Scene at the Second Picnic Day, May 3, 1910. *This event opened with addresses by the president of the University of California and of Stanford, a sign of a significance that has long since faded. On the hospitality side, the university provided free "coffee with cream and sugar," but "each guest should bring a cup and spoon." (UC Davis Special Collections.)*

5. 1. *Looking North, Second and G, c. 1928.* The Davis Arch, which was to the left, is now gone, but the Terminal Cafe (and Hotel) Building, on the right, has appeared. Over the 1920s and 1930s, this restaurant was a favorite meeting place of prominent Davis people. (California Promotion Collection, UC Davis Special Collections.)

5. 2. *Davis Civic Leaders,* c. 1920. The names of these four men are written at the bottom of the photograph. Their occupations are, from the left: large acreage farmer, garage owner, banker, retailer. The famous Davis Arch is to the right. (Hattie Weber Museum.)

5. 3. *Street Scene, 1922.* *Looking north along E toward Second (crossing on the right), we see the past and future next to each other. An automobile service station (Fred's Tire Shop) is on the left. Luft's Blacksmith and Horseshoe is on the right. The street is unpaved. (Ray A. Warner.)*

5. 4. *Growing Food in World War I.* *Food supply was a matter of great concern in The Great War. Among other programs, public school students planted "Freedom Gardens" on school grounds. (Hattie Weber Museum.)*

Picture 5. 5. is in the frontispiece.

5. 6. *Picnic Day*, c. 1919. *In the early years, Picnic Day automobiles parked on the campus "quad" and the open fields to the west of it. (Larkey Collection.)*

5. 7. *Judge Scott "Lays Down the Law" for Police Chief Floyd Gattrell*, c. .1928. *They are in front of the* Enterprise *building at 303 G Street. The windows contain reflections of a camera crew taking this picture and the two businesses across the street. (Larkey Collection.)*

5. 8. *Aerial View of College Park Looking North, 1940.* *Formed outside the Davis city limits in 1923, homes here were constructed at a slow pace. In this year, it was still only about two-thirds built-out. (Larkey Collection.)*

5. 9. *George Washington Pierce and Hiram Johnson, 1922.* *Pierce is second from the left and Johnson, in front, is on the right. The other two gentlemen are officials of the California Almond Exchange, where they are assembled. Pierce is 72 years old at this time. (Pierce Collection, UC Davis Special Collections.)*

Number of Homes Built in Davis Each Year, 1911-1938

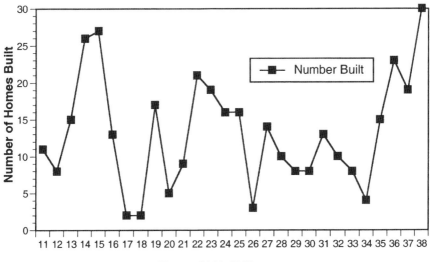

5. 10. *Homes Built in Davis, 1911–1938.* Edwin McBride kept a list of homes built in Davis from 1911 to 1938. This chart shows the number for each year. The ups and downs reveal World War I, the Great Depression, and the advent of federal home mortgage insurance in the 1930s. (Hattie Weber Museum.)

6. 1. *Davis Looking East, c. 1939.* College Park is seen in the lower left and the UC Davis Quad is in the lower right. This view shows how very small Davis was even on the eve of World War II. (UC Davis Special Collections photograph #3789.)

6. 2. Davis at Quintessential Small Town Development, 1945. *Jarvie Eastman, the Susanville, California postcard manufacturer, made this photograph into a postcard that sold well and widely. (UC Davis Special Collections, Eastman B-4705.)*

6. 3. Downtown Davis, 1941. *The intersection of Second and G is in the foreground. The abrupt transition from commercial structures to homes north of Third and west of F is striking. (Larkey Collection.)*

6. 4. "Main Street" Davis, c. 1940. *In the year 2000, only six of the 19 buildings seen here still stood. A large portion of them on the right were torn down in order to create a parking lot. (David Herbst.)*

6. 5. Wong Yee (left) and So Ho ("Louie") Young and their Children in their Sacramento Cafe, 217 G Street, c. 1936. *The Youngs operated this restaurant from 1918 to 1957, retiring after their youngest child (in Mrs. Young's arms) went off to college at UC Berkeley. (Marie Wong.)*

6. 6. Night Scene of Russell Boulevard Turning Right to Become B Street, c. 1930. *On the left, a billboard advertises the Hotel Senator. The Highway Garage is to the right of the billboard. Both are on land that would become the Davis City Park in 1937. (Isabel Sparks.)*

6. 7. The Davis City Hall and Fire Department, September 28, 1938. *In 1981, city functions moved to the 1927 high school, which had been refitted as a city hall. This became the "old city hall" and housed the Davis Police Department until 2001. (UC Davis Special Collections.)*

#104 CUSPIDOR, STEEL OLIVE GREEN FINISH.
18 SUNRUCA RUBBER CUSPIDOR MAT, GREEN.

6. 8. *Cuspidor and Mat for City Hall, 1938.* *Tobacco chewers attending city hall functions needed to spit. Therefore, a set of cuspidors with rubber mats were among the initial furnishings of the building. (City of Davis Collection, UC Davis Special Collections.)*

6. 9. *Davis Lumber Moderne Building, 1936.* *This building still stands, wonderfully restored, at the southeast corner of Third and G Streets. (Hattie Weber Museum).*

6. 10. Davis City Council, 1938. *This was the first—and the only—official photograph of council members before 1966. The picture was assembled in 1940 as a way to commemorate the construction of City Hall in 1938 as much as to memorialize the council. (City of Davis.)*

6. 11. Davis Volunteer Fire Department, Early 1938. *In September of this year, these firefighters would move to the fire department wing of the new City Hall. Here they are assembled in front of their quarters at 206 F Street. (Hattie Weber Museum.)*

6. 12. *Prominent Davis Males Playing Cards*, c. 1930. *Group on the left: C.A. Maghetti, Gordon Anderson, Sam Brinley, Sam Beckett, Ted Barger, Edwin McBride. Group on the right: C.F. Dixon, Forrest A. Plant, Dr. Wilfred Robbins, Ira Smith, Clarence Williams, Dr. Thomas Cooper (in center). (Westgate Collection, UC Davis Special Collections.)*

6. 13. *SP Depot Agent Sam Brinley Mock-admonishing* Enterprise *Editor Chelso Maghetti to Work Sundays on the Railroad.* *This photograph is one of several staged by SP photographers for media distribution. (Hattie Weber Museum.)*

7. 1. Near West Davis, c. 1950. *Russell Boulevard runs east-west across the bottom. The dirt road to the left, running north, will become Anderson Road. The home under construction in the lower right is 514 Campus Way. (UC Davis Special Collections.)*

7. 2. Brinley Building Under Construction, Northeast Corner of Second and E, 1963. *The Weber mansion shown in picture 3.5 has been demolished to make way for this building. (John W. Brinley.)*

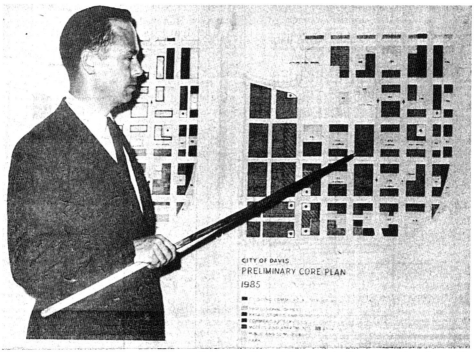

CITY PLANNER John Blayney, of Livingston and Blayney, points to a map which envisions the "core area" of the City of Davis as it can and may be in 1985 .if definite planning is done and carried out, step by step.

A capacity crowd of citizens gathered in city hall Tuesday night to hear the planning firm's preliminary report and recommendations on a core area survey which is costing a little more than $25,000 from equal contributions from the city and the state and federal governments.

The map shows existing commercial structures, professional offices, retail stores and offices, commercial services, motels and apartments, public and semi-public buildings and parks, and off-street parking lots as they would be in 1985 if the plan is carried out.

The pointer's end is on the intersection of E and 3rd streets, almost exact center of the core area under consideration. Third street, East-West, is designated as a mall-type "parade" probably for exclusive bicycle and pedestrian use and leading into the heart of the core area from the University campus.

(Harry Low Photo)

7. 3. Core Area Plan Presented, 1961. *(2, May 18, 1961.)*

7. 4. Looking North up G Street, 1965. *On the right, the Terminal Hotel has been "town and countyized" by constructing a "western" shade structure on its G Street facade. (Yolo County Historical Society.)*

7. 5. Stanley Davis "Alpine" Tract Home. *Tract homes such as this proliferated in Davis in the 1960s and 1970s. The glass doors in the garage tell us that this is the sales model. (2, May 12, 1964.)*

7. 6. Birch Lane Elementary School, c. 1966. *Many public schools were constructed in rapid succession in the "exploding" period. (Larkey Collection.)*

7. 7. UC Davis Dorms, Later 1960s. *UC Davis assumed responsibility for housing only a minority of its students on campus, but this still required many new dorms. (Larkey Collection.)*

7. 8. London Double-Deck Buses, 1968. *The city of Davis was slow off the dime on public transportation and the UCD student government started a bus system that featured real London double-deck busses. The advertisement on the bus on the left reads "McCarthy for President." (Larkey Collection.)*

7. 9. *Davis Bike Lanes, Later 1960s.* *By 1970, the major streets of Davis had bikeway signs. These signs indicated the presence of slightly less than auto-width lanes that some newcomers misperceived as too-narrow car lanes. (Larkey Collection.)*

7. 10. *UC Davis Exhibit at the Yolo County Fair, c. 1965.* *The social and cultural upheavals of the 1960s did not immediately bring the then-existing gender relations into question. (Yolo County Archives.)*

7. 11. *Vietnam War Support, November 1965.* *Prior to the "revolution of '72," the dominant ethos of Davis was conservative. Here we see merchants supporting the war in Vietnam. (2, November 19, 1965.)*

OLD GLORY—This is a section of G Street where Davis merchants displayed the flag today to represent their support of the U. S. government's policy in Vietnam. The display was throughout the entire business district and will continue Saturday.

DAVISVILLE '68 Distribution of first-edition copies DAVISVILLE '68, the recently published centennial history of the City of Davis, was facilitated by hard-working members of the Treasure Valley 4-H club of Davis, who spent most of last weekend wrapping corrigated paper around some 180 copies of the 240-page volume and carefully inserting them in book mailers. Those who assisted this community service project are l. to r., Theresa Gilliland, Bill Schlabes, Barbara Cameron, Allen Fleming, Jeff Whitehead, Jim and Nancy Schlabes and Alex Cameron. Not pictured, Cynthia Quinn.

Davisville distribution starts

The long-awaited publication of DAVISVILLE '68, The History and Heritage of the City of Davis became a reality on December 5, 1969, it has been announced by the Davis Historical and Landmarks Commission. Copies are being distributed this week to persons who placed the first 230 orders for the centennial publication. Some 80 additional pre-publication orders will hopefully be filled in about ten days, after which announcement will be made of several local distribution outlets.

In the meantime, Mrs. Walter Schlabes, the commission's distribution chairman, has stressed that mail orders may still be sent to the Davis City Hall, 226 F Street, Davis, California 95616. Checks should be made payable to City of Davis, Centennial Publication, in the amount of $6.80 (inc., tax & postage); or $6.30, plus a self-addressed envelope if they wish to pick up their own copies. Please, no phone orders!

The Historical commission has also rendered a commendable public service by individually wrapping and packaging for mailing some 180 copies of DAVISVILLE '68 last weekend. Mrs. Schlabes and Nelva Fairbrother, secretary to the city manager, attached the address labels on Monday and the books were all in the mail Tuesday morning. All who arranged to pick up their copies at the city hall have also been notified by telephone or mail. Those who have not yet heard are on the next mailing list and their indulgence is solicited.

"This final stage in book publication cannot be hurried," reports Mrs. Schlabes, who toured the facilities of the Anguin Book Bindery at Pacific Union College, near Calistoga, last Friday.

7. 12. *Larkey, Davisville '68 Published.* (2, December 11, 1969.)

93

Tonight at 8:00,
the polls close
for two years.

You still have a chance
to decide to direct
the changes that
will affect you.

You can do it now.

Bob Black
today

8. 1. *Bob Black Campaign Ad,* **Davis Enterprise,** *April 11, 1972.* *As UCD student body president and afterwards, Bob Black was a leader of the Davis version of the '60s quest for alternatives to a mainstream society that had discredited itself in racial matters, in Vietnam, and in other areas.*

8. 2. 1972–1974 *Skinner Davis City Council. This group was otherwise termed the "revolution of '72" council. Left to right: Bob Black, Richard Holdstock, Maynard Skinner, Joan Poulos, Richard Weinstock. (City of Davis.)*

Dear Davis resident,

As we move into 1978, it is with the encouragement of another year of demonstrated energy savings behind us. During 1977, the electricity consumption of the average Davis energy user dropped by nearly 6 percent, while natural gas use dropped by over 9 percent per customer.*

At the same time, the rest of the country has focused on Davis as a source of innovation and inspiration in the field of energy conservation. **Newsweek, Sunset Magazine** and CBS Television have been here to see what our city has to offer the rest of the world.

What is it we've got, and more importantly, what can we do to keep it going?

Well, we think what we've got, primarily, is you — concerned, enlightened citizens willing to make some personal sacrifices for the good of the community. Of course, as a city council, we're not as strange a group of bedfellows as we might appear, but our stand on energy conservation in new construction, in subdivision design, commercial landscaping, and in a continuing recycling effort — none of these would have stood the test of time without your support.

As for how to continue our progress in energy savings, **we** can only urge you to keep doing more of the same. By keeping thermostats down and lights off when not in use; restricting the use of household appliances; insulating those older homes;

and by limiting your automobile use by carpooling and by doing as much of your business as possible right here in town, we can all help to lower our energy consumption even further.

The world is watching now, so let's keep up the good work!

With best wishes for a happy and healthy 1978,

THE DAVIS CITY COUNCIL

*Figures based on information provided by the Davis office of PG&E.

8. 3. Energy Conservation Championed by the Council. *Promotional item in the Winter, 1978 city of Davis "energy conservation newsletter,"* Under the Sun. *(Lynn Campbell.)*

8. 4. Homes and Landscaping in Village Homes. *I asked Village Homes developer Mike Corbett to loan me photographs he thought best captured his fabled neighborhood. The five he very generously shared highlighted landscapes rather than structures. The above is my favorite among them. (Mike Corbett.)*

8. 5. *Worker-Members of the Blue Mango Cooperative Restaurant, c. 1983.* The Blue Mango *was one of a number of surging cooperatives in Davis in the early 1980s. Started in 1979, the Mango closed in 1994. (Jon Li.)*

CHEERING, hooting and calling out advise and comments, an overflow City Hall crowd awaited the Chuck Swift decision. Microphones were used so people stuffed in the hallway could hear the Council's opinons on patriotism and use of the flag.

Enterprise photos

8. 6. The American Flag at a Car Dealership, 1974. *A car dealer's proposal to display a huge American flag over his lot came before the council in January 1974. A large and demonstrative crowd turned out to support the proposal (which was approved). (2, January 29, 1974.)*

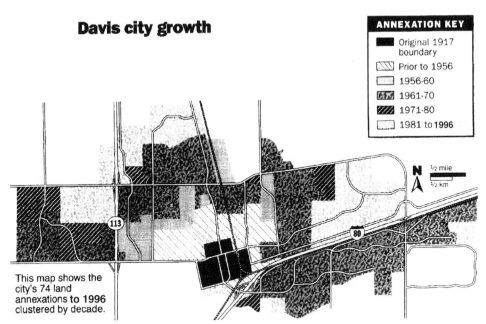

Davis city growth

ANNEXATION KEY

- Original 1917 boundary
- Prior to 1956
- 1956-60
- 1961-70
- 1971-80
- 1981 to 1996

½ mile
½ km

This map shows the city's 74 land annexations to 1996 clustered by decade.

9. 1. *Annexations to Davis, 1917–1996.* *(Nathaniel Levine graphic in 2, October 4, 1996, slightly edited.)*

9. 2. *1992–1994 Wolk Davis City Council.* *This was a tone-setting moderate council of the early "contested" period. Left to right: Dave Rosenberg, Susie Boyd, Lois Wolk, Julie Partansky, and Maynard Skinner. (City of Davis.)*

9. 3. 1998–2000 Partansky Davis City Council. *Green Party member and Davis Mayor Julie Partansky was a signal figure in the contested period. Left to right: Ken Wagstaff, Sheryl Freeman, Julie Partansky, Susie Boyd, and Stan Forbes. (City of Davis.)*

9. 4. Two Century-turning, High-rise Buildings, 2004. *After a long period of inactivity, the Natsoulas Gallery at First and E (on the left) and the Lofts (on the right) were among a number of multi-story commercial structures built in the Downtown near the turn of the century. (John Lofland.)*

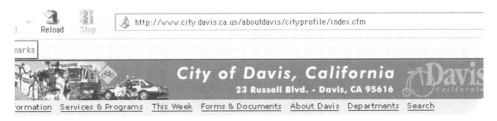

Profile

City of Davis Profile

Davis is a university-oriented city with a progressive, vigorous community noted for its small-town style, energy conservation, environmental programs, parks, preservation of trees, red double-decker London buses, bicycles, and the quality of its educational institutions.

9. 5. *Invoking the Past to Shape the Future, Spring 2004. This is a screen shot of the first section of the City of Davis web site profile of the community. Crafted by city promotional specialists, this opening passage assembles history-resonant images into a Davis-booster portrait.*

9. 6. *Debut of the Davis Toad at "Celebrate Davis," May 20, 2004. City promotional staff and business interests sought to make the toad a Davis symbol. Here, a city intern has the job of wearing the new, custom-constructed toad outfit. (John Lofland.)*

Historic hotel destroyed

9. 7. Davis Enterprise *Front Page Report on Demolishing the Terminal Hotel, September 19, 2000.* *This and related events led to strengthening Davis's demolition laws.*

75-year-old brick walls come down in 45 minutes

By Elisabeth Sherwin
Enterprise correspondent

On Monday morning a small group of people watched as the demolition of the city's historic downtown Terminal Hotel began.

It only took about 45 minutes for Stan Bowers of Valley Construction Co. to drive his excavator into the back of the 75-year-old brick hotel.

See HOTEL, Page A4

TUMBLING DOWN: The Terminal Hotel demolition began Monday. While the mural, above, cannot be saved, the bricks are being sold to the city. Mayor Ken Wagstaff hopes the bricks can be used in the site's new building.

Alison Portello/
Enterprise photos

9. 8. *Arch Mural Demolished, September 28, 2000.* *A mural of the Davis Arch painted on the north wall of the Terminal Hotel in 1976 became a Davis icon over subsequent years. It was "collateral damage" in the demolition of the hotel.* (John Lofland.)

Continued from page 64

Apparently, some crushed rock was finally spread on some streets in 1923 (7, p. 72). More than this, in 1924 many of the streets were truly paved and real sidewalks and curbs laid (2, March 7, 1924 and April 4, 1925).

Contour maps of pre-Davis and early Davis reveal that the initial street grid was sited over a swale—a water-carrying depression—that ran northeast from Putah Creek. It entered the grid at A and First and left it continuing northeast at Fifth and L. While not a "structure" in the ordinary sense, it was still very much a part of Davis life (and seen in the pictures on pages 72 and 81).

James Wilson, the first chair of the Davis Planning Commission in 1925, reported, "I, and many other people, got my car stuck trying to negotiate that thing in the wintertime. You'd get down in the bottom and you couldn't get out. You'd have to be pulled out" (Wilson in an interview with Larkey, 8, p.136).

There were also several other low points, especially in the railroad tracks' "Y." When it rained these and other locations filled with water and created what locals called "duck ponds." Excavation for the subway in 1917 created surplus dirt. In August of 1917, this dirt was offered free to residents. Editor Scott urged, "There are many pieces of property in the city which are low grade and now is the time to get dirt free for the hauling" (2, August 19, 1917; 8, p. 155).

Arch Demolished, 1924. Although apparently popular, the Davis Arch was taken down in 1924 because it obstructed a burgeoning new form of traffic: the automobile. Early drivers were apparently less skilled than today and kept running into it, making it expensive to maintain (7, p. 125).

When the Arch was about to be demolished on February 25, 1924, Judge Scott wrote a melancholy review of its life and troubles, concluding that "the fates decreed that it was merely a matter of the opportune time [until it came down and] the street paving proposition seemed to be that particular time. . . . Hence, Wednesday morning, Rodney Hill with a crew and tractor began the ghastly work" (2, February 29, 1924). (The Arch became a Davis icon and, in 1976, a mural of it was painted on the north wall of the Terminal Building. In ways not unlike the Arch, both the mural and the Terminal Building were demolished in 2000, as shown on page 100.)

Davis High School, 1927. Above, we saw that the formation of a high school district was hard fought. So, also, was building the actual school. The district having been formed, there were now debates over where the building should be, how it should be financed, and how it should be designed.

The ad hoc citizen's group that had purchased the block bounded by B and C and Fifth and Sixth had given it to the district. But this block was now seen as too small. The much larger tract west of it, called the "West Tranyham Tract," was available and better, in some views. That is where one now sees the building (which is currently the Davis City Hall).

Funding was the next problem. It was solved by a bond-issue vote of 427 to 40 in an election held on February 20, 1926. However, this seemingly ill-fated process then hit another snag. A technical problem was discovered and the election voided. It was held over and the bonds approved again on May 15, 1926.

Three hundred members of the Masonic Order were present for the building's cornerstone ceremony on February 19, 1927. The stone contained, among other items, a list of the names of the 39 residents who pledged money to buy the still unused lot for the high school. In addition, "the junior class planted a deodar cedar, which now towers over the southeast corner of the grounds," Larkey wrote in 1972 (8, p. 111; 14, p. 98). (As of the publication of this book, more than 30 years later, that cedar was still towering.)

Carquinez Strait Bridge, 1927. The opening of the "largest suspension bridge in the world" at the Carquinez Strait on May 21, 1927, was an important event for Davis and other places between Sacramento and San Francisco. It meant that the potential for automobile travel created by the 1916 Yolo Basin Causeway could now be more fully realized. Before the bridge, the road essentially stopped at the edge of the upper San Francisco Bay because, as reported, ferry services there were inferior to those at Oakland. Therefore, motorists commonly chose to go east or west from or to Sacramento by way of Livermore and Stockton.

The Carquinez Strait Bridge changed this, although the road itself was still meandering and not well paved. Nonetheless, the route was now more attractive and traffic through Davis began to increase. This increase stimulated auto-oriented businesses along the Olive-First-B-Russell route (to use their current names). By the mid-1920s, there was an auto court and campground on Olive and several gas stations on B.

Even before the Carquinez Bridge, auto traffic through Davis was rising. The *Enterprise* of August 29, 1924 printed a report claiming the Highway Commission had counted 35,000 cars in the 24 hours "a week ago Sunday." Writing in the *Enterprise* of September 17, 1925, Scott reported, "Mr. Hoag and three others are kept constantly on the go" with work at the Davis Garage, which was just south of the railway underpass.

Home Building, 1911–1938. Edwin McBride came to Davis in 1906 and was as an employee and then co-owner of Davis Lumber for 46 years. In 1917, he was among the five men elected to the founding Davis government, the board of trustees.

As someone who sold building supplies, he was interested in such matters as the number of structures constructed in Davis. In fact, he kept a "little black book" in which he entered the year, the name of the owner, and often the name of a builder of each new Davis home. He started this practice in 1911 and stopped after 1938 (although he did not die until 1954).

A typescript of this list was found in the archives of the Hattie Weber Museum of Davis. The list chronicled construction of 372 homes (plus 15 Asbill cabins constructed in 1936). Triangulating this 372 with other information we have on the number of Davis buildings, it appears that McBride made an at least near-accurate record of home-building over 1911 to 1938.

In this series, shown in the picture on page 81, we see that home-building clearly increased in the late restart period, 1911–1915. As World War I neared in 1916, the number began to fall and stayed very low (two per year) in 1917 and 1918.

Construction recovered after the war, peaked in 1922, and declined toward the end of the decade. Interestingly, the depression depressed home-building, but did not crush it. Indeed, it bounced back in the later depression years, peaking at 30 houses in 1938. The oddity of the late depression peak is explained by the New Deal advent of federal insurance for mortgages. Prior to the New Deal, home-building was made difficult by lenders' fears of buyer default. The New Deal allayed this problem by providing mortgage insurance. This reduced the risk of lending and stimulated home building. (For example, 648 D Street was built in 1938 with an FHA mortgage [11, pp. 131–133].)

Many other important structures were built, among them: *1919–1920*, the Davis grammar school burned down and another was built; *1920*, PG&E operations yard; *1921*, Varsity Theater; *1924*, Gieling Campground, Terminal Café Building, Davis Auto Camp ("Slatter's Court"); *1925*, Christian Science Church; *1926*, Presbyterian (Community) Church, Brinley Block Building; *1927*, Terminal Hotel, Boy Scout Cabin; and *1928*, Lincoln Highway Markers.

NEW CULTURE. The political culture of Davis was evolving in several ways.

The Populist Moment of 1917. The incorporation election of 1917 is sometimes characterized as a consensual event. The *Enterprise* headline announced, "Incorporation Wins by 3 to 1," meaning a vote of 221 to 87. This suggests a fair amount of agreement.

Five initial members of what was then a board of trustees were also elected and a similar consensus on them is sometimes implied. In fact, there was quite a diversity of opinion. Only the names of the five winners seemed to have been printed on the ballot. But this did not deter many of the 318 voters from writing in 57 other names. These 57 garnered 320 votes, which was 27 percent percent of votes cast (13, p. 13). While the five winners garnered 73 percent of all the votes cast and 56 percent of all possible votes—885 of 1205 and of 1590, respectively—there was also substantial dissent.

Consensus Politics, 1920s and Later. This "populous moment" was exactly that—a moment. The dissenters apparently saw that they were far from winning elections and stopped contending. I infer this from the fact that subsequent elections had very few candidates who were nearly always the same people and who got overwhelming percentages of the vote in low turnouts. Here are the results of the five regular elections for which there are data (from 13, p. 6, Table 1):

	# of Candidates	# Elected	Winning Percents	# Voting	% Turnout
1920:	3	3	96, 95, 93	95	22
1922:	5	2	87, 76	70	14
1924:	3	3	96, 94, 93	121	21
1926:	4	2	94, 86	70	12
1928:	3	3	100, 100, 98	52	9

Community Christianity, Early 1920s. In the early twentieth century, massive numbers of Americans left rural areas for cities. Some observers worried that this rush to Babylon meant American decay. One remedy was to strengthen rural life so that it could keep its youth "down on the farm." Protestant churches were especially active in this effort, among them the Federation of Churches of Christ in America. One of its strategies was to commission a series of "sociological" studies of successful rural churches that were intended to serve as models to follow in strengthening other churches and, therefore, their communities.

Among these was Edmund Brunner's edited *Churches of Distinction in Town and Country*, published in 1923. It consisted of 14 case studies of the "most successful" churches from around the nation. Chapter 10, by Marjorie Patten, was titled, "The Church at the Center—Davis, California." Apparently, Ms. Patten spent a week or so in Davis in 1921 or 1922 (the year is not clear) and concluded that the Presbyterian church under Reverend N.M. Fiske "has become the hub of a perfect wheel whose rim encircles the entire community with all its agencies" (19, p. 122).

She began her chapter by characterizing Davis people as highly individualistic before 1919 and Reverend Fiske's arrival. "Cooperative development was almost unknown [and] there was no special connecting link between the church and the community" (19, p. 123). But Reverend Fiske began tying his church "in some way to every agency in the village; and he determined to treat his problem as a business proposition."

Patten said his first step was to attend a meeting on Davis's sewage problems and to challenge those present to raise the $5,500 needed to construct a sewage system. The attendees took up the challenge. Fiske is said to have gone on to unite all the groups in the community in successful problem-solving in various areas. Organizations so dedicated included a Church's Ladies Aid and the Citizens' Class. The former was organized as a series of block divisions and captains that encompassed all of Davis, the author reported. The latter was composed of "nearly all the leading business and professional men of Davis" and numbered about 50 persons. This group apparently overlapped with the "Men's Class," which was Sunday school for civic-minded male Presbyterians. Reports of its meetings suggest that religion was studied less and issues facing Davis more. The program was typically organized around a guest speaker who talked about a "community development" topic.

According to James Wilson, who attended these meetings, then Mayor Gordon Anderson and soon-to-be Mayor Calvin Covell were especially prominent members. One of the first topics the group addressed was the need for Davis to have its own high school. This group was said to have done the detail work that made it possible to purchase a site on which to build a school (Wilson quoted in 8, p.136).

Patten ended her chapter by reporting that in the "last year" (1922?), 33 new people had joined the church, bringing total membership to 174. Thanks to Reverend Fiske, Davis was no longer a "sleepy little town." Instead there was evidence of a "big future [because people had] caught the vision [of a] progressive church [and were ready to] pull together [for] greater social, economic, educational, and religious development" (19, p. 134). "This work of the Kingdom [is] all one job," Reverend Fiske was quoted as saying, and people needed to stop "splitting it up into many jobs."

I do *not* summarize Ms. Patten's chapter as objective history (although it might be). Instead, I present it as an expression of a *cultural ideal* about "community Christianity" and small towns in this period. Specifically, Davis was thought to be an exemplar of this ideal.

It needs also to be understood that perhaps one-third of Davis's families belonged to the Catholic church. Its members included such prominent pioneer families as the Brinleys, Chiles, Dolcinis, Penas, and Webers. Over the 1920s, there was also a small but growing Christian Science congregation. All these people were likely outside Reverend Fiske's "perfect circle whose rim encircles the entire community."

Community Momentum, Later 1920s. The December 28, 1927, edition of the *Sacramento Bee* printed a feature article on Davis under the headline: "DAVIS ABANDONS LETHARGY AND IS IN FULL STRIDE TOWARD DEVELOPMENT." Its opening sentence reads, "After a slow period of development in civic affairs, Davis seems rather suddenly to have emerged into one of unusual growth." The body of the article enumerates evidences of "full stride": the Community Church, a gym for the new high school, a new University Farm building, the four-space Brinley block building, a second story on the Terminal building, a French laundry brick building at Third and G, and College Park.

Editor Scott reprinted the article with the demur that he was "not ready to concede" that Davis had been in lethargy. But he was clearly also pleased to reprint the article (8, p.159). This *Bee* article is of interest because it suggests how outsiders viewed Davis. They seemed to have sensed a new community momentum.

A General Plan, 1927. About 1923, civic-minded people began serious discussion of the possible need for a "city plan" (8, p. 134). C. Harold Hopkins—the then-owner of a tract of the previous LaRue ranch—even drew up a map of Davis as he envisioned it would be 25 years in the future. He presented it to the Men's Class on June 27, 1923, and the discussion there resulted in that group organizing several internal committees with titles like Community Plan of Improvement, Economic Welfare, and Health and Sanitation (8, p.126). The work of these committees led to a revision of the Hopkins map into a new map that was posted in both Davis banks in September 1923. Signed by the members of what was now called the Citizens Class of the Community Church, the text accompanying each map declared:

Homes Are Planned. Why Not Cities?

The time to make the plan is before the city has developed and grown. We all believe that Davis will some day become the center of a populous Agricultural and Educational Community. This plan is simply a suggestion of one of the many possible developments of

Davis. It is hoped that it will tend to focus the Community interest and arouse discussion on this subject (8, p. 127).

There was little further action for more than a year. Then in late 1924, Mr. Hopkins, who was still plugging away, took it upon himself to visit Mr. C. Harold Cheney in Los Angeles. Back in Davis, Hopkins represented Cheney as "one of the top-notchers" in architecture and city planning in whom he had stimulated an interest in Davis. Cheney was therefore willing to make "his fee extremely low [and come to Davis and] give the best he has in him in the way of city planning" (2, December 19, 1924; 8, p. 127).

The Business Men's Association then became involved and raised the "first $100 consulting fee" to bring Cheney to Davis (8, p. 133). He arrived on January 19, 1925, looked around the town, met with the board of trustees, and spoke at an evening banquet attended by "sixty representatives of local civic and fraternal organizations" at the newly completed Terminal Cafe (8, p. 134; 14, p. 40).

He told those assembled that planning was not merely a matter of "putting out a few trees and trying to make a show in front, but the question of your fundamental community building. . . . You have the opportunity now to take hold of your situation. This city is not spoiled very badly, nothing here is very alarming, but . . . " (8, p. 134)

People at this banquet adopted a resolution (offered by Dr. Bates) declaring that that "we are in favor of going ahead and having our city planned and all that follows it in the consequence" (8, p. 135).

On March 25, 1925, the board of trustees created a City Planning Commission that set about establishing zoning and starting to draw up Davis's first general plan (completed in 1927).

Why was a city planning commission created? When asked this question by Joann Larkey, the first planning commission chair, Professor James F. Wilson, answered:

> It was a combination of things. For instance, the fly problem in Davis was simply terrific because one could keep chickens, you could keep turkeys and cows. Many people did—right in town. Many other people thought you shouldn't have such things in town; and then the whole idea of city planning was taking hold all over the United States. It was a general movement so we adopted it. And right away some of the sanitary problems began to be solved (8, p. 136).

Professor Wilson also told Larkey that while he was in favor of a planning commission, he was surprised when he was "made chairman of it," although he then remained chair for some 12 years (8, p. 140). In this same 1972 interview, Wilson said of the 1920s:

> We did not have as many nor as vexing problems as the present city planning commission. Problems were very much simpler and we conceived it to be our first duty to examine whether or not the

> applicant's desire was going to hurt anybody. And if it didn't, he usually got his request. We served the public by insuring if anyone built a nice home no one else was going to establish a glue factory next door. Problems of that nature arose frequently (8, p. 136).

Wilson also agreed with Larkey that "the plan [of 1927] doesn't seem to have been carried out to any great extent. [Instead] the plan was implemented by a zoning ordinance and most of our effort was directed toward having people live up to that . . ." (8, p.140).

Other cultural matters of note in this period included the idea of a "purple circle" of pure breed livestock farms encircling Davis (early 1920s) (7, p. 23); the practice of solo and group singing at gatherings; and the changing of the names of the streets in the early 1920s.

* * *

In the vernacular phrase, Davis was "on a roll" from the end of World War I to the economic collapse of late 1929.

Chapter Six

DEPRESSION DAVIS, 1930–1945

The economic depression following 1929 threw Davis and the rest of the world into a well-known tailspin. It was the equally worldwide World War II that got both of them out of it. This chapter describes the Davis of this depression period.

QUIESCENT POLITICAL AND ECONOMIC LIFE. Davis seemed exuberantly boosteristic in the "urbanizing" period described in the previous chapter. Such enthusiasm prompted me to wonder how a new and bleak economic reality was received. Curious about how Davisites conceived the depression and its causes, I read the *Davis Enterprise* of the 1930s with particular attention to descriptions of it.

To my surprise, there was little on this topic under Scott's editorship before 1936 and under Chelso Maghetti's after that year. There were, though, backhanded mentions. On April 4, 1930, Scott penned a column titled, "Editor Sees Progress in Davis Life," which he began with "lest we forget, it seemeth [*sic*] well to direct the attention of our readers to the fact that . . . 'THE CITY OF DAVIS' is coming along fine. . . ." He then enumerates a number of Davis's positive economic, educational, and other aspects.

When a direct reference to the Depression was made, it likely took the form of "it's all in your mind," which was not far from Roosevelt's "we have nothing to fear but fear itself." In a talk to the Rotary Club on October 6, 1930, the editor and owner of the *Woodland Mail* proclaimed that "in his opinion the so-called business depression is largely a state of mind." The news report told us that "the speaker was highly complimented" (2, October 10, 1930).

My surmise is that this sparse reference to a major historical event suggests at least mild shock or denial. Some realities can be so inconsistent with one's world view as to be beyond the realm of mention. This does not mean the reality was not recognized. It was simply not spoken about, although certainly taken into account.

One form of this studied inattention was seen in Davis politics, which apparently went into retreat. In the earlier 1930s, *Enterprise* stories on council activities were brief or nonexistent. Council activities seemed few compared to the previous decade.

As can be seen below, council elections continued to have few candidates, consensual results, and low turnouts (except for 1940, when four seats unexpectedly came open at once). Indeed, there were no *Enterprise* reports of the 1932 and 1934 elections and, moreover, no known records of the numerical results *at all*. We only know who won by reports of who was sworn in for new terms:

	Number of Candidates	Number Elected	Winning Percents	Number Voting	Percent Turnout
1930:	2	2	100, 98	45	7
1932:	3	3	unknown	unknown	unknown
1934:	2	2	unknown	unknown	unknown
1936:	3	3	89, 87, 83	182	23
1938:	2	2	100, 83	102	11
1940:	7	3	85, 84, 44	507	49
1942:	2	2	100, 96	86	8
1944:	3	3	90, 89, 81	172	21

(from 13, p. 6)

It is perhaps of note that only two people (men) served as trustee president/council mayor between the first regular election of 1918 and 1946, a period close to 30 years. The first was A.G. (Gordon) Anderson, who served almost 13 years. He was succeeded by Calvin Covell, who served some 16 years (1931–1946, plus the additional year of 1917).

On the surface, life seemed simply to go on in Davis during the depression. On April 11, 1930, the Davis Chamber of Commerce published what seemed to be a self-congratulatory survey of the "business houses." Fifty-two of them had been counted, "with the average number of employees over three to each establishment, with the payroll approximating $190,000." These 52 were engaged in over 30 "different lines of business." Virtually all the business people lived in Davis and owned their own homes. All except two heads of business were members of the Chamber of Commerce. The Bank of Davis did fail in 1933, but this was attributed to frost in 1930 and a drought in 1931 that forced "farmers to withdraw their savings" (3, p. 28).

Suggestion of a certain coziness between the government and business in Davis was contained in the 1941 annual report of the Davis Chamber of Commerce: "Appreciation is expressed to Mayor C.A. Covell for allowing us to use his office for headquarters." It doesn't get much better than running a business promotion organization out of the mayor's city hall office.

WORKS PROGRESS ADMINISTRATION. The Works Progress Administration (WPA) was one of many "New Deal" Depression-fighting agencies. This one specialized in public works and favored projects that employed people over those that were land and materials intensive. Davis's project applications were apparently of the former sort.

With WPA funding, Davis Grammar (later Central) School was rebuilt as well as expanded in 1936. Aimed centrally at earthquake proofing, "the foundation and the ceilings are the same but the walls are of entirely new construction" (2, July 3, 1936, quoted in 8, p.149). An *Enterprise* report commented that "probably the most attractive room in the building is the auditorium, which covers a greater floor space than before. Decorative walls and ceilings add to the aesthetic appearance" (2, July 3, 1936).

Construction of Davis's first public park in 1937 was importantly funded by the WPA. Of the $13,128 total cost, the WPA contributed $8,355, leaving $4,773 for the city (2, February 21, 1936). (The dynamics of the park and its construction are described later in this chapter.)

In the later 1930s, the WPA placed concrete curbing on many Davis streets. The exact number is uncertain, but quite a few "WPA" initials followed by the year can still be seen on blocks within the 1917 (original) city. Among these, one each is in front of the Chen and the *Davis Enterprise* buildings (bearing the year 1938). Along Sixth Street in the Old North, several impressions read, "WPA 1939."

MORE STRUCTURES. The "golden age" described in the last chapter meant construction of many of what are now considered iconic and "historic resources." The depression slowed down, but did not stop construction of structures that would later be so regarded. Let me describe four and only list some others.

G Street Buildings, 1936. The *Enterprise* of September 25, 1936, reported that "the biggest building project that has ever occurred in the Davis business district will take place shortly when the east north half of G Street will be built solidly from the corner of Third Street to the Nicholson Chevrolet Garage."

Although America was still in serious (albeit recovering) depression, the owners of Davis Lumber were getting together with R.A. Wells to put up a structure that was one unit, but also "two distinct and separate buildings connected by a community wall . . . [and] owned separately." The building at the southeast corner of Second and G was retail space for Davis Lumber [235 G] and the structure next to it "will house four stores [228–234 G]" (see the picture on page 85).

Much was made of the building being "modern." And, indeed, the structure at the corner was restored to its original moderne splendor in the late 1990s. In another meaning of modern, the mid-1930s was still a period when heating and cooling were items meriting special description:

> [It will be] equipped with modern heating facilities for the winter months and an air-conditioning system for summer use. In addition to that, special insulation will be used . . . for the sole purpose of making the occupants as comfortable as possible the year round (2, September 25, 1936, quoted in 8, p. 152).

Davis City (Central) Park, 1937. Davis's first general plan (1927) called for a city park on the block bounded by Fourth, B, Fifth, and C Streets. It was finally built in 1937, but the process of getting there was long and required much effort.

Soon after the planning commission's creation in 1925, it began purchasing lots in that block. Among these was the southeast corner lot, for which it paid $450. At that time, the standard price for a Davis lot was $75 and certainly no one paid more than a $100. The commission was thus "roundly criticized for wasting taxpayers money," according to its longtime chair, Professor James Wilson (8, p. 140).

By the early 1930s, the commission had purchased most of the lots in that block, but a major problem remained. A.S. Nicolson's Chevrolet Garage stood on the lot "you see when you look straight down Russell boulevard into the park. . . . And there was a big electric sign out there that you could see for about four miles—'GARAGE' "(Wilson in 8, p. 140). In the 1930s, cars were still quite unreliable, so Mr. Nicholson did a thriving business with the heavy highway traffic passing that location. He had no incentive ever to move.

But fate of a sort intervened. The garage burned down in August 1934. Nicholson was persuaded to sell his lot to the city. In November 1935, a plan for the park was adopted by a joint meeting of the planning commission and the city council (8, p. 140).

A planning vision guided the commission in making this park a major project. According to chair Wilson, the orienting image was the view one would have when approaching the park from the west on Russell Boulevard.

> People coming down Russell Boulevard and looking ahead would see this greenbelt . . . and beyond that was the church [Davis Community Church] and next to the church (on the north) was to go the new county library. Then the new city hall was to be built [at the southwest corner of B and Fifth] (Wilson in 8, p. 140).

Central Park and Community Church were, of course, built and still exist, but the other two buildings and others projected in the 1927 plan never happened. And of course, the idea of a highway entrance to Davis along Russell became obsolete when Route 40 bypassed Davis in 1942.

As previously indicated, the park's construction was financed by local funds, volunteer labor, and the Work Progress Administration. Interestingly, in accepting WPA funds, the city had to agree to this provision:

> The W.P.A. is under no obligation to complete this project and should it become necessary for them to withdraw we agree to carry on the work to the extent that the project is not left in an unsightly or discreditable condition.

The statement was signed by Mayor Covell (City of Davis Collection, UCD Special Collections).

City Hall, 1938. As early at 1925, Davis movers and shakers had talked about and spun plans for a city hall. After all, the city council had to meet somewhere reasonably dignified. At the start, in 1917, the trustees had met in the county's jail-justice court building, but that burned down. Then it met "at various times in . . . the Masonic Lodge, Grady and Pugh's poolhall . . . and elsewhere" (8, p. 133).

As just mentioned, the first (1927) General Plan had placed the city hall at the southwest corner of B and Russell. But in a process that no one now recalls, the two lots at the southeast corner of Third and F became the place where it was actually constructed.

The cornerstone for it was laid on April 30, 1937. As with the high school building, Masons conducted the ceremony. "A record of the day's participants and events was sealed into the granite cornerstone" (7, p. 71). The finished city hall portion was dedicated on August 31, 1938. Designed in a "mission-style," the building was configured also to contain the Davis Fire Department. That portion was dedicated on September 17, 1938, in an event attended by some 200 fire chiefs who were holding a convention in Davis (7, p. 81; picture on page 84).

It is of note that its main room—the auditorium—was, according to James Wilson, "designed as a community hall where the whole population of Davis could convene. And it had a kitchen from which one could serve dinners to the people" (quoted in 8, p. 140). Among the items initially purchased to furnish the building were several "steel, olive green finish" cuspidors. Each of them sat on a green, rubber cuspidor mat (as shown in the picture on page 85).

The fact that Davis politics were consensual in this period does not mean that all the participants agreed on every course of action. Planning commissioner James Wilson reported that although he admired Mayor Calvin Covell, the two of them disagreed on building a city park and a city hall. Wilson wanted the former and not the latter and Covell was the reverse. According to Wilson,

> We went back and forth and back and forth. Finally he came to me and said, "What would it take to get you on my side?" I said, "It would take your boosting for a city park. And, in return, I'll boost your city hall." The result was we got both of them (quoted in 8, p. 140).

Impetus to build a municipal building was not only or merely a matter of civic pride or administrative convenience. As with the sewer system of the 1920s, state inspectors had shown up in Davis and declared the town backward. Previously, a major backwardness was sewage floating openly on city lots. Now it was a deplorable city jail. In the words of the state of California director of social welfare:

> This jail was built many years ago and is unfit for human habitation. It is a fire hazard to your community and is unsanitary and is in violation of both the Sanitary and Housing Laws of the State of California. I recommend that a new jail be built in Davis in accordance with the enclosed recommendations . . . (Florence Turner letter to C.A. Covell dated June 15, 1937, City of Davis Collection, UC Davis Special Collections).

The city council responded by turning the matter over to the county on the grounds that it, not Davis, owned the building. The council could not get off that easily, however. When the city hall was designed, it contained a jail that met state requirements.

State Highway Bypass, 1942. The opening of the Yolo Basin Causeway in 1916 and the Carquinez Strait Bridge in 1927 put Davis on the automobile map. Although the roads between Sacramento and the Bay Area were rough and winding, people were traveling them in ever-increasing numbers. On September 1, 1930, W.R. Russell sat on the porch of his home at the southeast corner of Third and B Streets and counted vehicles. He selected the five minutes between 11 and 11:05 a.m. and between 8:10 and 8:15 p.m. In the first five minutes, he counted 117 vehicles, which included five trucks and two buses. In the second five minutes, he counted 107 vehicles, including two trucks and one bus. This is a rate of just over 20 per minute. Editor Scott commented, "A rather busy highway" (2, September 5, 1930).

Further, a good part of this road through Davis was still unpaved in the early 1930s, creating unpleasant dust in summer and mud in winter. But, in the early 1930s, the roads along the streets now called Olive, First, B, and Russell were finally paved their full length and width. (As a state route, the state provided the bulk of the funding.)

In the 1930s, roads winding through towns and meandering across the countryside were increasingly perceived as torturously slow and uneconomic. Combined with a depression-prompted spurt of public works projects, heavily traveled winding roads were replaced by straighter highways. This was achieved by building entirely new roads outside towns. In the case of State Highway 40 through Davis, the straightening took the form of new road flanking Davis to the south beginning at what is now the east end of Olive Drive.

Opened on September 22, 1942, many Davis people perceived it as a blessing rather than an economic deprivation. Editor Maghetti editorialized in May 1941 that although the service stations would lose revenue, "along with whatever driblets accrue to the business firms in town, [the new road would eliminate the] juggernaut freight trucks, with open cut-outs and smelly exhausts, that thunder through all hours of the day and night. Their din is further accentuated by a heavy pull out of the subway, when the trucks begin to pick up their normal speeds again" (2, March 30, 1941).

In addition, the five automobile dealers and garage owners located on or near G Street had never been happy with what they thought were the business-draining gasoline stations on B. In 1934, five of them petitioned the city council to prohibit B Street garages from selling "any produces other than petroleum products." To allow them more would be to "split the business district . . . and lead to unfair practices and competition for business concerns on the main street [G Street]." In addition, "it would take money from Davis which belongs and should be kept in Davis" (Petition signed by the Liggett, Davis, and Varsity garages and by Nicholson Chevrolet and M.J. Fisher). These owners got their protection, but violations continued to be a threat. Finally, the 1942 state highway bypass greatly reduced out-of-town traffic, which solved their problem.

Physical structures and services increased a bit in the later Depression years: *1931*, St. James Catholic Church at Fifth and C built; *1938*, home delivery of mail began; *1941*, chamber of commerce offered low-price trees for planting in the strips between the sidewalks and the curbs and the trees became the property of the city that could only be removed for a "legitimate reason" (2, February 18, 1941); and a medical building for two physicians and two dentists constructed at 216–18 F Street, leaving the second floor of the Anderson Building empty "excepting for some rooms occupied as living quarters" (2, July 4, 1941).

WORLD WAR II DAVIS. World War II meant many new, albeit temporary, cultural and social practices. Orchestrated or demanded by federal or state authorities, Davisites seemed to regard these changes as positive duties rather than as onerous tasks.

War Activity Before December 7, 1941. The Japanese attack on Pearl Harbor on December 7, 1941 is often characterized as a "surprise." A sleeping America was "rudely awakened" into an unexpected war.

While the exact day and place of the start of World War II may have been a surprise, the imminence of war was not. For a considerable period prior to December 1941, the *Davis Enterprise* carried front-page reports of war preparations:

June 14, 1940:	Because of the "chaotic conditions of world affairs," the State of California asks people to conserve scrap iron.
July 5, 1940:	"The Mayor requested each member of the council to check with the employees of their divisions for absolute loyalty to the Government, an action that is coming universal over the country."
February 29, 1941:	"Davis Draftees Ordered to Active Service Next Week"
June 13, 1941:	"Gasolineless Sundays." "Sunday outings in the family car may be banned so that America's tanks . . . and battle cruisers may have heavy stores of reserves to meet any emergency."
July 25, 1941:	"In conjunction with hundreds of other communities over the United States, Davis will stage its drive for old aluminum beginning next Monday. . . ."
August 15, 1941:	"Freight traffic equal to pre-depression days is reported passing through the Davis station . . . Military requirements make up a large part of the freight increase . . . "
August 29, 1941:	"A drive is under way to secure members for a Home Guard unit for Davis. . . . The unit is to replace the National Guard, which has been called into active service."

An Observation Tower. In September 1941—three months before Pearl Harbor—a Ground Observer Corps was organized in Yolo County (2, September 19, 1941). An observation tower about twenty-five feet high was constructed at the northeastern corner of Fifth and B Streets and staffed by some 250 volunteers around the clock seven days a week. Their job was to identify and report all aircraft (8, p. 160).

Victory Gardens. While World War I had "Freedom Gardens," World War II had "Victory Gardens." This was a major effort in which every vacant lot in Davis was identified and the city council provided free water for gardens on them (8, p. 33; 7, p. 134). A contest for the best such garden was held among elementary school children and an evening class in "Home Gardens" was given at the high school in early 1943.

Campus Became a Signal Corps School. Ordinary college instruction was suspended and the campus became a U.S. Army Western Signal Corps School on February 1, 1943. Among other accoutrements, one building "bristled with antennae, transmitters, receivers. . . . [Young Hall was] the home of Radar, strictly G-2. A formidable sash of barbed wire was stretched about its girth, then placed under twenty-four hour armed guard" (quoted in 7, p. 97). Indeed, the military announced that commencing on Saturday, February 6, 1943, at noon, "the general public is excluded from the University Grounds until further notice" (2, February 5, 1943).

Control of the campus was returned on October 31, 1944. Classes resumed on a limited scale in early March 1945 and a full program was underway by October of the same year (2, March 16, 1945; 7, p. 98).

White Collar Men Did Manual Labor. Starting in 1942, "real" laborers were apparently in short supply because of military service. Rail tracks were deteriorating and freight was piling up, particularly at the Southern Pacific's Oakland terminal. SP issued a labor recruitment call to its station agents and Davis's Sam Brinley responded. Hoping to get college students, he found that they and others had already been recruited for agricultural work. Undaunted, he set about recruiting the deferred white collar males of the town to help " 'keep 'em rolling' for the national good" (8, p. 108).

About 100 such Davis men were recruited and their pictures and names featured prominently in the *Enterprise*. They went to Oakland and moved freight on Sunday, September 27, 1942, and on an unknown number of subsequent Sundays. Other station agents had also responded to the SP call and those from Davis worked alongside white-collar men from places like Palo Alto.

SP and the national media focused on this volunteering and promoted it as "The Davis Idea." It was featured in *Time* magazine's "Wartime Living" section on February 15, 1943 and *Collier's* dispatched a writer to Davis to interview participants. In addition, the SP took professionally staged and posed photos of a number of them acting like they were repairing tracks or about to do so. One was captioned, "Off to the Front," and featured four prominent men sitting on a rail utility cart staring grimly ahead as they were "leaving for the job 'somewhere on the right-of-way' " (8, p. 108; 7, p. 134; 2, February 19, 1943 and June 11, 1943).

Japanese "Internment" and Other Race Matters. In May and June of 1942, U.S. soldiers took more than a thousand Japanese people from their homes in Yolo County and imprisoned them at Tule Lake, California and other locations (9, p. 85–86). A small but unknown number of them lived in or near Davis.

On the broader subject of ethnic and race relations in Davis in the 1930s and 1940s, it would seem that there were too few non-Europeans to be able to speak of the town as having "interethnic" or "interracial" relations in the usual sense.

What scattered and few representatives of people of color there were seem to have been treated as acceptable exotics rather than as threatening outsiders. For example, the hardworking Louis Young family, who ran the Sacramento Cafe on G Street (serving an American, not Chinese, menu), seemed accepted, albeit accepted in its place. That is, except for the five children attending public schools, the family did not otherwise press for involvement in mainstream Davis. In addition, Mr. and Mrs. Young embraced the Americanization of their children. All five of them were given the first names of G Street merchants, a fact "everyone" knew and that signaled a "melting pot" mindset. (The names were Marie for Marie Rogers, Violet for Violet Gordon, Dell for Dell Grieve, Frank for Frank Cassiter, and Alice for Alice Brady. The first three were involved in the Red and White variety and grocery store, just a few doors north of the Young cafe. After the first child so named, it is said that G Street merchants jokingly admonished Mr. Young, "name the next one after me.")

Along this same line of dealing with acceptable exotics rather than threatening outsiders, we might consider the position of Davis African-American Austin Stafford. Mr. Stafford was the Red Cap at the Davis S.P. Depot from 1933 to at least the June 15, 1945 issue of the *Davis Enterprise* in which he was profiled (with a photograph) on the front page. Referred to as "Oscar" in his Red Cap role, the article characterized him as "popular with the passengers, his fellow workers at the depot, and all who know him. As the photo indicates when he smiles, he smiles all over and that is always the sign of a genial soul" (2, June 15, 1945).

In this period, some white merchants apparently believed that "Oriental" retailers competed unfairly against them by keep their stores open long hours and staffing them with low or unpaid family members. On January 26, 1940, this kind of fear prompted representatives of several Davis food stores to ask the chamber of commerce to speak with the city council to "prevent the opening of an oriental food store in Davis next month" (2, February 2, 1940).

The chamber responded that it was not legal to ban such a store, but that it would (and did) back an ordinance "regulating opening and closing hours" of food stores. Subsequently, the city council unanimously adopted such an ordinance. It regulated grocery, meat, and vegetable stores, but exempted "bakery shops, pool rooms, drug stores, restaurants and other businesses" (2, February 23, 1940).

Other stereotypes of racial and ethnic groups also seemed alive in Davis, including even the blackface minstrel show. The annual Faculty Club Goose

Stew of December 21, 1940 was organized on the theme of the Old South. "The Recreation Hall on the college campus was transformed Saturday to the dining room of an old southern plantation, with small bales of cotton and clusters of fruits and nuts decorating the long tables. . . . The stage was . . . flanked by cotton plants, and on the stage was a Negro shanty behind a picket fence."

After a number of dances done in "old southern plantation" costumes, the highlight of the program was a "minstrel show," for which W.W. Robbins was the interlocutor (2, December 27, 1940).

At the Council meeting of June 7, 1943, Mayor Covell expressed his support of Army General DeWitt's proposal not to allow Japanese nationals or citizens to return to California after the war. It died for lack of a second. Councilman B.A. Madson noted that it was likely unconstitutional to apply the policy to U.S. citizens.

There followed what the *Enterprise* called "considerable criticism and comment" over the Council's "failure to take a stand in favor of "the DeWitt proposal (2, June 18, 1943). Thusly encouraged, Mayor Covell called a special meeting for June 21 in which to consider a revision that applied only to Japanese nationals. It was adopted unanimously by the four members present (2, June 25, 1943).

Reports in the *Enterprise* chronicle a wide variety of other war-related activities, a few of which included: blackouts and a system of air-raid wardens to enforce them; collecting newspapers; rationing sugar; forming a disaster preparation organization; removing the name "Davis" from the PG&E warehouse and town water tank; conducting several "buy bonds" drives; activation of the Davis unit of the California State Guard; collection of junk metal; keeping the Davis High School closed an extra week in September 1942 so the students could pick tomatoes; consideration of having to "resort" to women letter carriers (in desperation, two were finally hired); and registration for Ration Book One and Ration Book Two.

CAMPUS CHANGES. On the all-important campus, there were changes, but not of the magnitude of the previous period. Aside from the suspension of instruction for World War II (described above), one of the more important changes was an elevation in its organization. In 1938, it went from the mere "Northern Branch" of the College of Agriculture at Berkeley to the College of Agriculture at Davis. As the agricultural faculty at Berkeley had feared from the start, the Davis folks were gaining on them. This name change was an important symbolic achievement in the process of moving toward both independence and equality.

As the national economy improved in the later years of the depression, more buildings were constructed: Hickey Gym in 1938 (with WPA funding), an enology laboratory (1939), an administration building in 1940 (now a part of the University Library), and a chemistry building in 1941 (Young Hall) (24, p. 50). Also, work on winemaking began (1935), teaching of home economics started (1936), and a veterinary school was authorized (1941), but not started until after World War II.

Before 1932, the Quad was seeded with barley or alfalfa, which produced real and practical harvests. In 1932, sprinklers were installed and lawn grass was sown and grown. This change was symbolic of a school on-the-make. In one stroke, its central place went from rural to urban, from farm to city, from hick to slick.

CULTURE. There were a number of interesting changes in and elaborations of the cultural life of Davis.

A New *Davis Enterprise* Editor, 1935. The remarkable William Henry Scott edited the *Davis Enterprise* as his private/public journal of Davis from 1899 to 1935. His personal imprint was so clear week after week and year after year that those of us who have read the paper extensively feel we almost came to know him.

Chelso Maghetti was Scott's successor. He had come "to Davis in 1919 and served as Postmaster from 1927 to 1936." Like Scott, he edited the paper with his personal stamp and for many years—25 in all (7, p. 111). And also like Scott, Maghetti was an ardent Davis "booster." Their editorial voices on this and related matters were sometimes so similar that one has to look at the date to be certain who wrote a given item.

Under Maghetti, the *Enterprise* remained conservative in spirit and Republican in politics. In editorials, he regularly railed against what he saw as immoral New Deal hamstringing of business. In his page two report of the 1944 Presidential contest, he tried to put the best face on a bad situation in saying the election was "not a total loss for Republicans in the Davis Community" because Dewey had bested Roosevelt by 25 votes (565 to 540) (2, November 17, 1944). (Nationally, Dewey lost to Roosevelt 46 percent to 53 percent.)

Scott turned 80 years old on November 28, 1941. This event became the occasion of a large noontime celebration conducted by the Rotary Club and accompanied by a "huge birthday cake" containing eight lighted candles. Scott's daughter had circumspectly researched and written his biography, which was read at the gathering and printed on the front page of the December 4, 1941 *Davis Enterprise*.

Smoking Banned in the City Hall Auditorium, 1940. In February 1940, the city council banned smoking in the City Hall Auditorium—the main room and where the council met. One might interpret this as an early sign of Davis's environmental and health consciousness, but that would be an error. Instead, in the little more than a year since the building's completion, "smokers have been careless with cigarettes. . . . Several burned spots testified to the damage done in the past." Therefore, smoking was banned in the Auditorium (but not, apparently, in other parts of the building) (2, February 23, 1940).

Gunfire Entertainment, 1940. On February 26, 1940, Miss Gloria Jacobs, age 17 and a resident of Woodland, addressed the regular noon meeting of the Davis Rotary Club. She spoke on how she came to be a "champion woman marksman" in pistol shooting and indicated that those interested could view an exhibit of her achievements in the window of the Davis Pharmacy. That exhibit contained 285 trophies, medals, and cups she had won for "perfect marksmanship" in contests held in many sections of the country. These awards included the title "Champion" over both men and women (2, February 23, 1940). In her talk, she showed the three pistols she used and explained the "perfect precision of their construction" (2, March 1, 1940).

At 1:15 p.m. the same day, she gave an exhibition of her marksmanship in the basement of the city hall, where a target had been set up. This was a previously announced public event, and a "large group of interested spectators" was reported to have been present. There, Miss Jabobs proceeded to shoot a "perfect score." Her father, who was also present, declared that her marksmanship greatly exceeded his own. It seems that he, Yolo County's highway patrol captain, was a pistol enthusiast who had tutored his daughter in this sport from the time she was age 12.

Bike Troubles, Early 1940s. In the later 1960s, Davis began a long-running love affair with the bicycle. One might therefore infer that this romance had deep roots. But this seems not to have been the case. In fact, it was the reverse. The *Davis Enterprise* of March 14, 1941 informed us that "the increasing violations of the bicycle ordinance and failure to secure licenses will bring citations in the future is the warning of the Police Department this week. . . . the continued riding of bicycles on the sidewalks has brought numerous complaints to the department . . . and a tightening up is in order. . . . [People who had not yet bought their 1941 licenses faced] confiscation of their property." Furthermore, it was illegal to ride a bike at night without a front light and a rear reflector. Those violators were also put on notice.

Bikes made the news again in February 1943 when the *Enterprise* admonished readers, "When you ride a bicycle you are part of traffic and must obey traffic laws, just as if you were driving a car" (2, February 19, 1943). There followed a detailed recitation of a biker's obligations. These included use of hand signals and not "hooking" a ride. The article further explained that new problems with bikes were arising because of the "great increase" in their use "particularly among adults as a means of wartime transportation."

As Davis moved into the 1950s, this perception of bikes as a problem in need of control continued. Rather like roaming livestock, bikes were an irksome or even dangerous presence on the streets and sidewalks.

Other cultural innovations of note in this period included the beginning of the still continuing Fourth of July Kiddies Parade in 1935, and the start of the annual Chamber of Commerce Covell Community Service Trophy award in 1944 (8, p. 109).

* * *

Before the end of World War II, Davis people were animated by visions of postwar growth and prosperity. In an editorial titled, "Looking Forward to a Post-War Project," *Enterprise* editor Maghetti opined on February 18, 1944:

> Following the conclusion of this war, by every estimate possible Davis is due to have a building boom to house dozens of additional

families that will want to come here to live or attend college, and if a similar pattern is followed like that which occurred following the first World War, attendance at the University will zoom to untouched figures to date. If we are forward looking, we will plan now to meet this need.

The Friday, August 17, 1945, issue of the *Davis Enterprise* carried a front page report of Tuesday's end of World War II celebration. On the same page, there was an account of the citizens' petition that would soon result in the first expansion of the town since its formation in 1917. A new world had started. Begun in the depression, it was underway well before World War II ended.

Chapter Seven

EXPLODING DAVIS, 1946–1971

The events of World War II destroyed the "old world," both literally and symbolically. The late 1940s were the beginning of a new world in the United States and elsewhere, an era of fresh starts, new enterprises, and rapid economic growth.

- In 1945, the territory of Davis was less than *half a square mile* and its population was about *2,500*.

- By 1970, its territory was over *six square miles* and its population was pushing *24,000*.

This was about a 12-fold increase in area and a ten-fold increase in population in a span of 25 years.

These two soaring numbers were of course accompanied by a great many other soaring numbers, such as those for houses, streets, schools, churches, businesses, and the like. This chapter displays these profound changes and some of the people and organizations who constructed them.

ANNEXATIONS. By 2004, the city of Davis had carried out 79 annexations (including the incorporation "annexation" of 1917). That first action created a place four-tenths of one square mile. The 79th—in July 2001—brought Davis to 9.9 square miles. The *pace* of expansion is shown when we divide the 79 into the five periods in which they took place:

Period	# of Annexations	Square Miles Added
Urbanizing (1917–1929)	1	.4
Depression (1930–1945)	0	0
Exploding (1946–1971)	50	5.8
Progressive (1972–1989)	16	2.3
Contested (1990–)	12	1.4
TOTAL	**79**	**9.9**

It is clear that the number of annexations and square mile growth were concentrated in the 1946–1971 period.

Among the annexations of this period, the 1,006 acres that created a "South Davis" in 1966 is of special note (#34 in the city's numbering). It is the single largest annexation in the city's history. With it alone, Davis's square miles went from 3.0 to 4.6. This huge enlargement was not animated by proactive optimism or a positive vision of a new and wonderful "South Davis." Instead, it was a defensive counter-move against a developer who had organized a subdivision in Yolo County several miles southeast of Davis. Called "El Macero" (a pseudo-Spanish label), it was an upscale suburban tract built around a country club and golf course. Not yet a municipality, Council members feared it might become one and a "twin city" that would compete with Davis. Hence, the strategy was to take control of the land between Davis and El Macero as a way to limit the latter's capacity to grow if it did incorporate.

UNIVERSITY GROWTH AND STUDENT UNREST. The major engine of Davis's growth was, of course, the University of California.

Student enrollments soared. By 1949, the Davis campus was the fastest growing of all UC campuses. From barely 1,000 students in 1945, there would be some 13,000 (and steadily climbing) in the early 1970s

Territorially, the campus became much larger and buildings proliferated, these among them: *1959*, Robbins Hall, Hoagland Hall, Voorhies Hall, and Wickson Hall; *1961*, Memorial Union Assembly (later Freeborn) Hall; *1963*, Olson, Sproul, and Hutchinson; *1964*, agricultural toxicology facility; *1965*, Physical Sciences Building II, Primate Center; *1966*, Mrak Hall and Bainer Hall, Shields Library tripled in size with a new wing; *1968*, Storer Hall; *1969*, Wellman Hall and Kerr Hall.

Units of instruction and research proliferated. These were among the major, new units: *1948*, School of Veterinary Medicine; *1951*, College of Letters and Science; *1961*, Graduate Division; *1962*, College of Engineering; *1964*, School of Law; *1966*, School of Medicine;*1967*, the College of Agriculture renamed College of Agriculture and Environmental Sciences; *1970*, Veterinary Medical Teaching Hospital opened.

In the period immediately after World War II and up to the later 1960s, the "agricultural sciences were blessed with large infusions of federal and state money. . . . The Davis campus benefited dramatically. In less than ten years its land holdings tripled and new buildings and laboratories rose one after another. [These included] million dollar homes for the plant sciences, food technology, and home economics" (24, p. 86).

All of the above was undergirded by the state's adoption, in 1959, of the famous "master plan" of higher education in California. In a sharp break with the past, this plan systemized postsecondary education by creating a three-tier structure in which the University of California was a lofty "research university." Davis was included as a relatively minor unit in this top tier. Earlier this same year, the Regents conferred the status of "general campus" on Davis, a change that the master plan affirmed. This brought UCD into the magic circle of nine campuses making up the largest and most prestigious research university in the world (24, p. 106).

DAVIS

UC Davis now had the authority to propose and, with Regents' approval, establish new majors, schools, and colleges, as well as to carry on many other activities without oversight by Berkeley. Begun in 1906 as a bleak patch on which to tinker with plants and animals, it finally reached the top in 1959. But the *real* competition had now begun. No longer a country cousin that hardly counted, it began to play on the same field as Berkeley and UCLA—and Harvard and Yale. It had jumped from the top of the small time to the bottom of the big time.

It would be a mistake to think of the growth of UC Davis or Davis as special. In fact, both explosions were typical of the time. Both were instances of the wider phenomena of massive growth in post–World War II California and higher education in America. The national explosion of higher education is particularly relevant. In a 2001 *New York Review of Books* essay, Louis Menand characterizes 1945–1975 as "the golden age" of colleges.

> The number of American undergraduates increased by almost 500 percent and the number of graduate students increased by nearly 900 percent. In the 1960s alone, enrollments more than doubled from 3.5 million to just under 8 million; the number of doctorates awarded annually tripled; and more faculty were hired than had been hired in the entire 325-year history of American higher education to that point. At the height of the expansion, between 1965 and 1972, new community college campuses were opening in the United States at the rate of one every week (18, p. 44).

Menand points to three factors as fueling this enormous growth: "the baby boom, the fairly sustained high domestic economic growth rate after 1948, and the cold war." As described in the next chapter, these and other factors began to change in the early 1970s, ending the "Golden Age" of the American college. And with these changes, Davis changed.

The exploding period of Davis history encompassed three generations, or "types," of college students: the older and more serious GI bill students of the 1940s, the silent generation and "organizational man" students of the 1950s, and the rebellious, anti-Vietnam/anti-establishment students of the 1960s.

Davis had the first two types in abundance. They formed the dominant culture of the campus in their respective periods. UCD did not, however, have many of the third type of student in the 1960s. Several bizarre assassinations combined with the insanity of Vietnam drove many 1960s students to despair and rebellion. In contrast, Davis students were remarkably quiet and even pliant. Mike Fitch captures this nicely:

> Despite their close historical ties, UCD and UC Berkeley couldn't have been more different in how they adapted to the hippie era. Berkeley became a hotbed of cultural revolution, while Davis, by and large, stuck to the straight and narrow, becoming a safe haven for students wanting to escape the craziness of the 1960s, a place where

conservative parents could send their kids without worrying too much (4, ch. 1, p. 2).

According to the official history of UC Davis, the quietness of Davis students was in part due to then Chancellor Emil Mrak's fielding of a program called "Project Involvement" in the later 1960s. It was "designed to defuse some of the tension" by having campus officials meet with and listen to students in an almost unending marathon of talk (24, p. 145).

Even so, in 1966 a student named Bob Black was elected ASUCD president "on what he viewed as a 'mandate for radical change' in student government at Davis" (24, p. 143). Under his leadership, student government moved into new areas, including initiating a double-decker bus system to transport students to and from the campus, bringing left-leaning speakers on serious issues to campus, and founding the Experimental College. The campus organic community gardens grew from the milieu of this period, as did the Whole Earth Festival.

FROM "BUSINESS DISTRICT" TO "CORE AREA." In a great many if not most American towns and cities, rapid expansion of retailing and services over the 1940s and 1960s took the form of encouraging (or at least allowing) peripheral shopping malls that had the effect of drawing business away from and ultimately decimating traditional downtowns. The three-part complex of (1) the dead downtown, (2) the highway retail strip, and (3) the large shopping mall at the edge of or outside town is a virtually defining feature of the American landscape.

The Downtown "Saved." The economic and political elites of Davis reacted differently. The G Street business crowd early on viewed growth as a threat to them. While they favored rapid *residential* growth at the edges of the town, they saw that large-scale retail at the periphery would undercut them. Indeed, this threat was so obvious to them and spoken about so often in the pages of the *Davis Enterprise* that I have wondered why elites in other towns did not more often react like those in Davis.

One reason for this difference may have resided in the nature of the Davis downtown as compared to some others. That "nature" must be understood in the context of the nature of Davis itself in 1945.

In that year, Davis, including its downtown, was *very small*. As indicated, its population of 2,500 mostly fit into about half of a square mile. The entire town barely spanned six blocks north to south and twelve blocks east to west.

The "downtown" of the late 1940s was little more than one (or perhaps portions of a few) of the some 70 blocks making up the whole town. This is easily seen in the picture on page 82 that shows the entire downtown in 1941. The abrupt transition from commercial to residential shown in the upper portion of that photo is particularly striking.

In a strict and traditional sense, when people speak of "saving" Davis's downtown they should be speaking only about the few blocks at and contiguous with G and Second Streets. However, the "downtown" that people commonly now think as having been "saved" refers to that area in only a minor way. Instead, the geographic referent has become, to a great extent, what was previously much of the entire town.

This shift in meaning and referent started in the late 1950s and early 1960s. At that time, "downtown" became a large part of the 24 blocks bounded by First and Fifth and B and G. Many of these residential blocks were redefined as commercial blocks and, therefore, as the "downtown." The upshot was that Davis not so much "saved" its downtown (i.e., the immediate Second and G area) as it started over and built an entirely new downtown on ground to the north and west of the tiny old downtown.

By 1970, the planned and official "center" of the downtown had shifted two blocks west and one block north—from Second and G to near Third and E. Second Street was displaced as the main corridor from the train station to the UC campus and replaced by Third Street, which was thought to be a possible "parade" shopping mall. (For want of owner cooperation and financing, this mall/parade never happened.)

A Hip "Core Area." One can well ask, "How did all this happen?" The short answer is that the public and private political and economic elites formed a funding partnership that hired a San Francisco planning firm to create a plan for a new downtown. Significantly, the firm was provided a fairly detailed set of guidelines that were developed by a 50-member Core Area Citizen's Advisory Committee (2, February 2, 1961).

Pictured on page 89, John Blayney of the firm of Livingston and Blayney is giving a public lecture on May 16, 1961 on the just-delivered plan. The photograph's caption sums up the plan nicely: almost complete, large-scale reconstruction of residential areas adjacent to the old downtown and a Davis population of 75,000 by 1985.

The term "core area" that became standard in the Davis lexicon (meaning roughly the new, 24-block "downtown") was introduced by this planning firm. Indeed, their plan was titled *Davis Core Area Plan* (10). In this period, *Davis Enterprise* editors often put quotes around "core area," suggesting that it was an odd (or at least novel) expression.

On reflection, Livingston and Blayney renaming much of the original Davis as the Core Area was quite clever. By means of this they sidestepped issues of what one really meant by "downtown" or "business district." Instead, one was talking about something new: the CORE AREA. And rather like converts to other causes, Davis elites perhaps rejected their "old fashioned, downtown" selves and embraced a shiny new Core Area self.

Demolition of the Existing Town. If one was going to build a new downtown/Core Area consisting of Corbusier-style high-rises surrounded by large parking lots (which is what the plan showed in its schematics), then one has to get rid of the old town. And this Davis did—with seeming vengeance.

Curious about just how thorough the demolitionists of the 1950s–1970s had been, in January, 2000 I used the 1945 Sanborn fire insurance map of Davis to count how many of the 1945 buildings were standing in 2000. In 1945, the entire town had 583 buildings (excluding garages and such). In

January, 2000, I counted 330 buildings as still there, a survival rate of 57 percent (12, p. 7).

However, the survival rates of the town's four areas were quite different. If the "downtown" is defined as the 24 blocks bounded by First and Fifth and B and G, 86 of the 233 1945 buildings had survived to the year 2000, a survival rate of only 37 percent. This was much lower than the survival rates of the other three areas, which were 82 percent, 62 percent, and 54 percent (of the Old North, University-Rice, and the Old East, respectively) (12, p. 7).

Decline of the Original Downtown. In the 1950s, Davis's original "Main Street" (G Street) had become an embarrassment to local elites. In his 1959 farewell speech to the Chamber of Commerce, departing city administrator Frank Fargo admonished the assembled business leaders, "You must clean up G Street, make it look more modern." The news report on this luncheon continued:

> One guest in the audience said, "G Street now looks like the backdrop for a western TV show." Another said, "Why not an editorial about our business section called "Gunfight at the Bar B Saloon" (2, January 15, 1959).

Fargo further proclaimed, "You need to get your redevelopment plan going. It is vital. New businesses won't move into an area that is so run down."

In a speech to the Davis area Chamber of Commerce in January 1961, planning consultant Lawrence Livingston declared, "the downtown Davis appearance is not too attractive. . . . [Davis lacks] the special character of a college town center" (2, January 19, 1961). The February 1961 report of the Core Area Citizen's Advisory Committee characterized the business district as "presently drab and uninviting" (2, February 2, 1961).

Redevelopment actions in the key 200 block of G Street included tearing down most of the buildings on its east side, just north of the Terminal Hotel building. True to form, the open space created by demolition was made into a parking lot. In addition, almost half the buildings on the west side of G were demolished and replaced. But these actions were not enough to turn things around. The G Street part of the "downtown" drifted without clear character or identity. (Portions of the text above are adapted from 14, pp. 59–94.)

CONTROL OF PERIPHERAL RETAIL.

The obvious flip-side of a sustained downtown was control of retail at the periphery. The idea, however, was not to prohibit it. Instead, shopping areas would be kept small in number and at "neighborhood scale." Four of these were planned and built: University Mall on Russell in 1965; G Street center north of Fifth in 1967; Davis Manor on Eighth Street in 1969; and Lucky's Center at Anderson and Covell in 1971. Additional centers were resisted.

CITY GOVERNMENT GROWTH AND CHANGE.

The city government struggled to keep some sort of order while providing amenities amid all this change and growth.

Facilities. Dotting the landscape with thousands of new homes and other buildings required a massive expansion of the sewer and water lines, much of which was carried out in the mid-1960s. Units of city and county government multiplied and/or underwent significant growth. These changes included: *1962* and subsequent years, neighborhood parks in East and West Davis, 26-acre community park at Fourteenth and B Streets; *1966,* new fire department headquarters completed; *1967,* community park and pool opened; *1968,* new county library building on Fourteenth Street opened.

Consensus Politics Eroded. In the chapters on urbanizing and depression Davis, we saw that City Council elections were remarkably "consensual." Few candidates ran, they were elected with large majorities, and few people voted. This pattern eroded over the 13 elections of this period. Here are the lowest winning percentages and the highest percentage received in the elections of 1946 through 1970.

Election Year	Lowest Winning Perent	Highest Percent
1946	62	76
1948	54	64
1950	77	69
1952	65	72
1954	75	84
1956	**46**	55
1958	57	63
1960	53	56
1962	**48**	52
1964	52	61
1966	60	68
1968	**45**	**47**
1970	**47**	57

(Winning office with less than 50% of the vote shown in boldface.)

Excepting the atypical election of 1940, the trend to electing people with less than a majority vote dated from 1956. It then happened four more times in this period. Also, in 1968, the highest vote-receiver garnered less than a majority for the first time. This was Vigus Asmundson, who was also the first mayor with less than majority support (47 percent), but only the first of many to come. (He may also have been the last Davis politician who dared tell a reporter that the group who met with him and asked him to run included "one of the city's leading developers and the head of Wells Fargo Bank's local branch"[4, ch. 2].)

Emblematic of this erosion, the champion of consensus politics, Calvin Covell, retired from the council in 1947, one year into his fifth term. He had been elected in 1946 with 62 percent of the vote and had run second for the two open seats in a three-man race. This was in contrast with three previous wins in which he had finished first with 100 percent of the vote every time. (The numerical results of the 1934 election he won are not known.) Perhaps he felt he had lost public support and it was therefore time to quit. (Covell had served continuously as mayor since 1931—a remarkable 16 years plus one year as president of the trustees in 1917, giving him 17 total years.)

Old-Timers and Newcomers. The enormous increases in population reported in the opening sentences of this chapter had implications for the political makeup of the electorate. Members of this horde of newcomers tended to conceive of themselves as more modern than old-time Davis people and more cosmopolitan than the locals. A great portion of them were UC Davis faculty and administrators and their families. More liberal than the "downtown crowd" and the "old aggie" faculty, they began to think of reform and responsible government. However, like the old-timers, they also tended to embrace rapid growth.

A sense of the need to prepare for a new era was expressed in the formation of a Davis chapter of the League of Women Voters. Among other innovations, the league organized the first public debate among city council candidates (a practice that then became standard in Davis political life).

In this shifting political milieu, in 1958, Kathleen C. Green became the first woman ever to run for city council—and she won. Some viewed her election as a turning point in the process of wresting control of the Council from the old-fashioned downtown and aggie-faculty crowds. It opened the way to the election of many more newcomer cosmopolitans, who included Clyde Jacobs (elected 1960, a professor of political science), Norman Woodbury (elected 1960, 1966, and 1970, a Sacramento lobbyist for municipal utilities), and Maynard Skinner (elected 1966, a UCD administrator).

As one might predict, numerically overcome by this flood of reform-minded new residents, some among the downtown and aggie-faculty groupings were dismayed and a few were embittered. An old order was passing.

COMMUNITY ORGANIZATIONS PROLIFERATED. As a human population grows, one sign of its social strength or weakness is the degree to which people organize themselves into non-, quasi-, or extra-governmental associations aimed at achieving community purposes. I think we can say that the burgeoning population of Davis exhibited considerable strength in this way. Without attempting to enumerate every civic association created in this period, let me indicate some of the more important of them.

A large number of new Davis people had children and seemed to think that one good way to educate them was to put them in publicly financed schools. Vote after vote on school financing was successful, resulting in a landscape dotted with new school buildings. These included: *1945*, Emerson Intermediate School (now the school district headquarters); *1954*, East Davis (now Valley Oak), West Davis Elementary; *1957*, North Davis Elementary; *1960*, Davis Senior High; *1962*, Birch Lane Elementary (seen in the picture on page 90); *1966*, Pioneer Elementary, Oliver Wendall Homes Junior High (and Central School razed); *1967*, West Davis Intermediate School (now Robert Willett).

Over its first six periods (1868–1945), Davis had only three churches with much longevity: Presbyterian and Catholic (both formed in the early years) and Christian Science (formed in the 1920s). This began to change in 1946 when the Church of Christ and the Davis Lutheran Church started to organize. A cascade of others followed, including the Episcopal Church of St. Martin in 1953. The Catholics were refounded in the sense of moving to much enlarged quarters that included a new St. James Church at 14 and B Streets in 1967. Writing in 1968, Joann Larkey (7, p. 107) reported "today, twenty-one churches, embracing many faiths, are currently listed . . . "

Much of the usual assortment of service and civic groups came into being: *1945*, Davis Lions Club; *1947*, American Field Service, Veterans of Foreign Wars; *1954*, Soroptimist Club of Davis; *1955*, Davis Jaycees; *1957*, Camp Fire Girls, League of Woman Voters of Davis; *1958*, Davis Kiwanis Club; *1959*, the Davis Art Center, Davis Chamber of Commerce became the Davis Area Chamber of Commerce, Friends of the Davis Library (successor to the Library Club); *1962*, Davis Family Services League, Davis Jaycettes.

Among other community organizations, there was the special case of the Davis Community Hospital, which opened in February 1968. Before that year, Davis residents in need of hospitalization had to travel to Woodland, Sacramento, or farther afield.

CIVIC CULTURE. People do not live by organizations alone, a misimpression this chapter might so far convey. They also live by ideas, ideals, and inspiring symbols of community identity, among other cultural matters. Two cultural topics stand out in this period.

Identity-Challenge and the Bicycle. In early 1953, the Chamber of Commerce board of directors decided that Davis needed a slogan and an "emblem." The implication was that Davis had neither at that time. It was, so to speak, identity-challenged.

The Chamber's strategy for acquiring both of these was to hold a "contest of real interest" in which people submitted proposals. The prizes were $25 each for the slogan and the emblem. The *Enterprise* reported that "the winners will be announced at the 4th of July program in the City Park" (2, March 30, 1953). However, the contest apparently did not produce acceptable results. So far as I can tell, winners were never announced and no slogan or emblem was adopted.

Moving toward the 1960s, the city remained identity-challenged. In the same period, bicycles not only continued to be common on Davis streets but also grew in numbers. Recall from the last chapter that bike riding caught on during World War II when it was a practical alternative to the auto because of gas rationing. Bike habits learned during the war survived it. As the city grew but was not yet large, bikes were popular among high school and college students, as well as among adults.

Chapter Seven: Exploding Davis, 1946–1971

Indeed, there so many bicycles on the sidewalks and streets that they were considered a nuisance (if not a menace). The February 20, 1964, *Enterprise* featured pictures of mothers pushing babies in strollers at the edge of the sidewalk at the corner of Second and E Streets, apparently having trouble using the walk because of bikes. The photos were captioned: "Why the Detour? . . . because walking on downtown Davis sidewalks is something akin to a basic training obstacle course. That's why." A number of people began to demand that something be done to control sidewalk and street obstruction—and chaos. Matters continued to be problematic and in December 1965, the chief of police announced a "get-tough bike policy," which was a "crash program of citing violators" using "special teams of officers in the field" (2, December 17, 1965).

At this announcement, the chief also "expressed doubts about establishing bike paths," an idea that had been presented in a petition to the Council a year earlier. Containing 533 signatures and given to the Council on December 10, 1964, it called for "bicycle paths on all arterial streets [and] parking areas in shopping centers." Eve Child, spouse of UCD economics professor Frank Child, had been the moving spirit in drafting and circulating the petition, assisted by like-minded friends and neighbors. In a February, 2004 interview, Frank Child told me that although Eve was the strategist and driving force for the bike lane idea, she insisted that he—not she—speak for the cause in public. According to fellow activist Dale Lott, Frank was "tall, distinguished and spoke with a confident, relaxed baritone," reasons, perhaps, that Eve Child wanted him to represent the cause (2, July 27, 2003). (The Childs had recently returned from living in the Hague, a place where bicycles were a serious form of transportation, complete with bike lanes. As put in the headline of a September 30, 1976 *Daily Democrat* story on the couple, "They Brought Holland to Davis.")

In the same interview, Professor Child related that "people laughed at us" in response to early presentations to the Council. Dale Lott also participated in these early efforts and recalled that Council members "stared at us incredulously." As the group persisted, the response became hostile, Lott reported (2, July 27, 2003). But the committee did not quit. After more than a year, on April 11, 1966, the Council grudgingly authorized a "pilot program" of a few lanes on small, side streets. This was unacceptable.

The spring of 1966 was also council election time. Of the three men running, Davis newcomer and UCD administrator Maynard Skinner strongly endorsed a robust bike lane system. He was elected. At the council meeting of September 26, 1966, he led the authorization of a wide-ranging and *arterial* system. Thus began what would become a major system of bike lanes. As Lott related it, "At the end of the meeting, city staff was directed to meet with our committee and design bike lanes. We danced out of City Hall" (2, July 27, 2003).

Identity-challenged Davis had finally found its emblem and, more broadly, its identity. It was no longer a vague and drab old-fashioned place. It was "THE CITY OF BICYLES" and "The Bicycle Capital of the World" (8, p.

79). Business and other organizations soon began using bike logos on their materials. With city approval, in 1968 the Jaycees put up street signs declaring "CAUTION [Image of a bike] HOME OF 18,000 BIKES" (2, March 28, 1968). Joann Larkey's centennial Davis history book, published in 1969, featured a high-wheeler bicycle logo on the front cover (7). This logo was itself the city's "official centennial emblem." It had been selected in a contest held by the Chamber of Commerce Centennial Committee using the criteria that the emblem-idea had to represent "the most unique aspect of life in Davis" (2, April 12, 1968).

Recall that in 1953, this same Chamber of Commerce held a Davis emblem contest in which there was no winner, perhaps because there was no "unique aspect of life in Davis." Now, 15 years later, such an aspect had finally been found—or should I say invented? All of this was deeply ironic in view of the fact that only three years earlier the Davis establishment was anti-bicycle.

So, Davis made lemonade from lemons with bikes. One interesting sidelight is that such lanes were not then legal in California. The State Vehicle Code had to be amended to allow them (7, p. 79). A second interesting aspect is that bike lanes became an integral feature of both on-street and off-street development. In 2004, 51 of the 157 miles of streets in Davis had bike lanes, almost one-third. There were an additional 51 miles of off-street paths routed through the city's extensive internal system of "greenbelt" parks. These meandering green-strip parks were themselves in part inspired by a vision of city-wide bike transportation.

Another Identity-Challenge: "Canning?—in Davis?" In August 1956, Hunt Foods, Inc. announced it was purchasing a large site at the northeast corner of the railroad and Covell Boulevard on which to build a "food processing plant" (aka a canning factory). Given major, front-page space in the *Davis Enterprise* of August 30, 1956, this was the opening move in what would become one of the more protracted and bitter of Davis's community conflicts.

In the space of under a year, Davisites would vote four times and campaign in three elections on questions of allowing the plant and under what conditions. At least two levels of factors were at work in explaining this intense brouhaha.

The *first* level involved the political maneuvering engaged in by the City Council. A citizen's group naming itself the Cannery Referendum Committee (CRC) formed just after the Hunt announcement and started an initiative petition. The initiative set standards of industrial performance and of waste disposal guaranteeing that the city would not lose money on *any* new plant or subsidize one. It soon had more than 800 signatures and was close to qualifying for the ballot. Before it did, the council organized a "straw poll" on the plant, per se, one without specific text on such standards. It set the vote for November 6, the day of the Eisenhower-Stevenson presidential election. The result was 55 percent pro-Hunt, 33 percent against, and 12 percent not voting on the Hunt matter (2, November 8, 1956). (For context, consider that Eisenhower won with 59 percent in Davis and with 57 percent nationwide.)

Pointing out that the vote was on the plant as an idea and not on the CRC initiative, the group pressed ahead in trying to qualify it for the ballot. Again the Council preempted the initiative with its own, now official election, on Hunt. Held on January 14, 1957, the result was 55 percent to 45 percent in favor of the Hunt plant (2, January 17, 1957). Not yet having had its day in court, the CRC once again pressed on, finally qualifying the initiative for a special election. The Council set it for July 16, 1957. However, the Council also placed its own less stringent (in some eyes) version on the same ballot. The pro-Hunt forces won both propositions. The CRC initiative failed 42 percent to 56 percent. The alternative Council proposition won 41 percent to 58 percent (2, July 18, 1957).

The *second* level of explanation involved the technical pros and cons of the plant and, beyond these, the class nature and identity implications of a canning plant in Davis. From the start, the City Council, the Chamber of Commerce, and allied interests were enthusiastic supporters of the plant. They stressed the importance of Davis moving away from its then heavy reliance on residential property taxes for pubic services. They claimed that the plant would pay far more taxes than it would cost the city. Other people were not so certain. Such a plant produced considerable waste that was costly to manage. What would processing the waste cost and who would pay? In addition, the plant was seasonal and would be at capacity between July and October. This would involve 1,100 temporary employees. From where would they come, where would they live, and what impact would their children have on the schools?

In an informational and debate meeting in October 1956, Dr. Thomas Cooper and others asked about the health aspects of "a transient-type population," especially as regarded immunizations and handling tuberculous cases. Dr. Walter S. Tyler asked this audience "if they would let the children of the migrant element sit next to their own children in the city schools." Further, the increased demand for housing "created in the surrounding area" would surely mean that "slums will pile up" (2, October 11, 1956). In an anti-Hunt ad published in the October 11, 1956 *Enterprise*, reference was made to packing "our already over-crowded schools" and attracting "large numbers of cannery workers" who would "camp around Davis." The plant would create "a public health menace and an all-around headache."

It was clear in the *Enterprise* reports just quoted and in many others that a considerable element of social class protectionism was operating in resistance to the Hunt plant. In suggesting this, I do not question the validity of the main anti-Hunt claim that the plant would cost the city far more in services that it would ever produce in taxes. This could have been a valid argument at the same time that class protectionism was also at work.

Ironically, it was the traditionally conservative Davis groups that held the inclusiveness/diversity/compassion high ground. The pro-Hunt position minimized negative impacts on the public schools, housing, and public health. One such argument was that most Hunt workers would be people already in Davis, such as wives of townspeople and students. There would be few migrant workers. Even if there were, Dean of the College of Agriculture Fred Briggs declared, "We're an educational community. Maybe we ought to take on the job of educating these kids and improving the health of migrant workers. If we can't then there is no reason for . . . smugness" (2, October 11, 1956).

More broadly and deeply, the issue could be seen as one of, "What is Davis, anyway?" Dean Briggs caught hold of this question when he asked, "Are we through with the job after producing our crops? Who's going to can the tomatoes? Apparently we think we are a little too good for that. How do we differ from Winters and other towns?" For at least 40 percent of Davisites the answer seemed to be that Davis *was* different from Winters and other towns.

It was an identity defining moment, but the identity defined may not have been one either side anticipated or wanted. Perhaps the identity acquired was that of a fractious place that seekers of new plant sites would do well to avoid. In this sense, the anti-Hunt forces may have won the war even as they lost the battle. Subsequent decades did not feature more serious overtures from such plants or battles over them. (Instead, the battles revolved around real estate proposals and their taxes, which was the future the pro-Hunt forces feared.)

In this unplanned way, Davis got a canning factory, but the consequences of the battle began to move it to being a clean, upscale "University City." Years ago, a Berkeley dairy used what was then the humorous slogan: "Farms?—in Berkeley?" After some decades and today, people might say with humor, "Canning?—in Davis?" But, in 1957, such a slogan was not funny.

In mid-1957, Hunt had permission to build its plant, but it did not do so for another three years. In that interval, it openly pursued siting elsewhere. Apparently unable to find a better deal, it started construction in the summer of 1960 and began operations in the 1961 season.

* * *

In his 1998 book on Davis, *Growing Pains*, journalist Mike Fitch suggested that many of the major themes seen in the exploding period continued right through subsequent decades. I think his elaboration of that point is accurate and serves to amplify the overarching theme of "radical changes, deep constants."

> Ironically, many issues that made headlines during the 1990s already were hot topics of discussion in 1968. Something had to be done about the narrow Richards Boulevard underpass. The downtown needed to bolster its retail base, parking remained a problem and merchants worried about threats from peripheral shopping centers. At UC Davis, students had to worry about talk of fee increases. Parents of teen-agers were being told they had to face up to the community's drug problems. Residents resisted efforts to increase their taxes. City officials talked about the need for low-cost housing (4, ch. 1, p. 3).

Chapter Eight

PROGRESSIVE DAVIS, 1972–1989

In the postwar period, Davis was only another exploding California town. Hundreds of Bill Streng and Stanley Davis tract homes were expanding its borders. Despite the bicycle, Davis as a truly distinctive locale was not yet born.

But born it was. In the span of less than two decades over the 1970s and 1980s, Davis developed the distinctive image of being

> a community that's enlightened, progressive, environmentally aware. It embraced growth control as gospel, saw the sun as an energy source and began singing the praises of recycling long before most communities. It's a nuke-free, pro-choice city that declared itself a sanctuary for political refugees from Central America. . . . (4, Introduction, p. 1).

This was, of course, only the boosteristic (or "progressive") version of Davis's new distinctiveness. Responding to the same changes, there was also a detractor or evil twin distinctiveness in which Davis was "eccentric" and "self-absorbed" (4, Introduction, p. 1). To detractors, Davis was negatively distinctive in having "an overabundance of middle-class high-achievers out to save the world. Failing that, they at least want to save Davis from urban sprawl, suburban shopping malls, the world's love affair with automobiles and other affliction of the modern world" (4, Introduction, p. 1). Favorite detractor catch-phrases born of this period, and continuing, included, "Only in Davis," "Carmel By the Causeway," and "the People's Republic of Davis." *Enterprise* columnist Bob Dunning's appellation was perhaps the most famous: "The City of All Things Right and Relevant."

This chapter tells the story of how Davis went from dumpy nothingness with a little bike emblem in 1971 to progressive glamour, celebrity lovers, and hostile detractors by the late 1980s.

THE "REVOLUTION" OF 1972. I cautiously fix the birth of "progressive Davis" as the evening of Tuesday, April 11, 1972. That night, the votes counted in the City Council election made it clear that the order of things in Davis was changing in dramatic ways. None of the three winners was from the old downtown or UC aggie circles, the traditional sources of Council members. Nor were they clearly in the mainstream of the newcomer "modernist" elements described in the last chapter. Indeed, the only incumbent standing for reelection—classic "old boy" Harry Miller—received only 33 percent of the vote, running far behind the third-place finisher (Bob Black) who had 59 percent.

Poulos, Holdstock, Black. The three elected were, instead, from new kinds of constituencies representing new ideas. Finishing first with 74 percent (a strength not seen since 1954 and never again even approached) was Joan Poulos. She was a 35-year-old attorney and mother of two who had not lived in Davis long and who had come to town with her spouse, a professor of law in the new School of Law. In second place with 68 percent was British-born Richard Holdstock, liberal Democratic activist and director of environmental health at UC Davis. Last but certainly not least was Bob Black with 59 percent. A recent president of the UC Davis student body, he was at this time part-owner of an organic/health food store in Davis (one of the first in the U.S.).

All three represented the "newcomer cosmopolitans" described in the last chapter. Within this broad tendency, however, there were differences on the questions of how rapidly Davis ought to grow and in what fashion; the degree of acceptance of traditional white male leadership; and the support, or lack thereof, for the Vietnam War and the broader cultural challenges of the time.

The cosmopolitans newly dominant in the late 1950s and 1960s envisioned rapid growth and reconstructing Davis's downtown as a series of Corbusier–style high-rises and parking lots (4; 11, pp. 48–49). However, by the early 1970s, consequences of this rapid growth were visible and stirred misgivings. Growth then became an issue in the 1972 election.

Of the nine candidates, Poulos, Holdstock and Black seemed most clearly to catch hold of the problems. These three did more than politically question the dominant, growth-oriented cosmopolitans. Their physical appearances questioned it in other ways. With the exception of Kathleen C. Green, elected in 1958, council members were male. Moreover, these males were clean-shaven, short-haired, and coat-and-tie wearing. More recent candidates were more cosmopolitan and liberal, but were nonetheless "old-fashioned." Poulos, Holdstock, and Black were otherwise: a woman, two males with beards (one of whom wore hippie-like garb, long hair, and no coat or tie, as seen in the pictures on page 94). In 1972, changing a City Council was a public ritual of literal replacement.

> They began the meeting with a table full of business-looking men, all clean-shaven, wearing suits and ties. . . . [The men who replaced them] were bearded, one had long hair and both wore short-sleeve shirts, and there was a woman. For me it was a visual representation of the change . . . and it was very potent and very charging (Mickey Barlow, quoted in 13, p. 16).

A Precarious Progressive Majority. When we look at the election results of the progressive period, we see further erosion of old-time consensus politics. Progressive candidates were elected with enough frequency to form working majorities. But, with the exception of 1972, they did not dominate elections.

This precariousness can be thought of in two parts. The *first* part involved the continuing decline in lowest-winning percentages and the highest percent of votes received. These were the figures.

Election Year	Lowest Winning Perent	Highest Percent
1972	59	74
1974	**37**	**40**
1976	**33**	50
1978	**48**	49
1980	**48**	62
1982	**45**	**46**
1984	**45**	**46**
1986	51	53
1988	**42**	51

(Winning office with less than 50% of the vote shown in boldface type.)

Of the 26 people elected in the previous—the exploding—period, five were voted for by less than a majority, which is 19 percent. The voting results given above present a very different picture. Among the 18 elected, 11 had less than a majority, which is 61 percent.

The *second* part of understanding the progressive's precarious hold on power is to inspect the ideological leanings of the 13 people elected to the council in this period in relation to their strength in elections. In time-sequence, these people won office with *the lowest-winning percents:* Bob Black, Tom Tomasi, Sandy Motley, Tom Tomasi, Bill Kopper, Tom Tomasi, Gerald Adler, Ann Evans, and David Rosenberg. Also in time-sequence, these people received the *highest percentage* of votes: Joan Poulos, Jim Stevens, Bob Black, Jim Stevens, Sandy Motley, Ann Evans, Debbie Taggart, Mike Corbett, and Mayard Skinner.

In most standard assessments of these matters, Black, Tomasi, and Kopper were considered the most liberal-minded of Davis's elected officials. They also ran among the weakest in the elections they won. In contrast, arch-conservative Jim Stevens was the highest vote-getter *twice* in the heydays of the progressive period (although he was denied any serious service as mayor by progressive majorities). Poulos, Motley, Evans, Taggart, Corbett, and Skinner were ambiguously mild leftist or centrist, and all often did quite well.

I conclude that while the political leadership of this famous progressive period could achieve majorities sufficient to adopt innovative policies, its dominance was precarious. However, it was a precariousness of an odd sort because the electorate was also rather liberal on national and state issues. McGovern rather than Nixon easily carried Davis in 1972; Proposition 13 was decisively rejected in 1978; Reagan failed to carry Davis in 1980 and 1984; Republican Governor George Deukmejian lost in Davis in 1982; and voters retained Chief Supreme Court Justice Rose Bird in 1986 despite her defeat statewide. Such a pattern suggests that the center of the Davis electorate was liberal, but, locally at least, in a centrist manner. Thus, center-moderates such as Polulos, Motley, and Taggart did well at the polls. The precariousness involved people further left, such as Kopper, Tomasi, and Black.

Sources of the "Revolution." A change of this kind invites speculation on its causes. In his *Growing Pains*, Mike Fitch suggests a number of "forces at work," which include the following. (1) The entire country was in a crisis of the legitimacy of authority as well as subject to other profound changes. In that context, more people were ready to look at new alternatives. (2) Davis was growing at a rate that was making even conservatives nervous. It had added 2,000 people in 1971 alone. (3) The existing council was in disarray. Two of the three incumbents up for election did not run. Another had announced that, for personal reasons, he was resigning and leaving town after the election. (4) This was the first election in which students could vote. They were an estimated 3,400 new voters in a community where people were previously elected to office with some 2,300 votes. Because the three winners ran strong in *all* precincts (not just "student" ones) election pundits have disagreed on how important these new voters actually were. Nonetheless, students did vote in very significant numbers. Almost 5,000 people voted in 1968 and 4,300 in 1970. These numbers were doubled in 1972: 10,957 (which would prove to be the largest number up to the 1980 election). (5) Using the initiative process, a UC Davis student had organized a successful campaign to place a peace proposition on the ballot. It called for an immediate withdrawal from Vietnam and placing domestic goals above military involvement in other countries. This alone was thought to have brought out voters, especially student voters. The initiative carried with 76 perent. (Three bond issues funding public amenities also passed with large majorities.)

GROWTH CONTROL. Before the election in 1972, the Vigus Asmundson Council had appointed a citizens' task force to begin revision of the city's general plan. The new plan adopted in the following year limited and controlled the city's future growth. Some characterized it as a "radical step" because, at that time, Petaluma was the only other California town that had tried to impose growth limits. The plan required that growth be limited to that required to meet "internally generated" housing needs (4, ch. 2). "The main tool" for doing this was a system of yearly "housing allocations" (4, ch. 2). Starting with allocations in the 300 range, in December 1975 the council cut it to a maximum of 150 single-family houses in the next year. This was done "because Davis is growing too fast" (3, p. 35).

The housing allocation number was geared to projected desirable population levels. The early-on target was no more than 50,000 people by 1990. In 1981, the council voted to change it to 50,000 by 2000.

As the 1980s moved on, external pressures to grow mounted. In 1987, a new revision of the General Plan was begun. In December of that year, the plan was amended to state that Davis would grow at 1.78 percent per year. This would result in a population of between 72,000 and 76,000 in 2010.

A "hot" housing market in Davis began to encourage speculators to buy houses for the purpose of using them as rentals. Some people thought that the sale—and often the resale—involved in this process increased both rents and the sale prices of houses. Seeking to curb such supposed upward pressure, in July 1977, the Council passed a law requiring that all buyers of single-family homes "guarantee to live in the house for one year following its purchase" (3, p. 35). (The measure contained a 1981 "sunset" clause and was not reenacted.)

In spite of growth control efforts, 1977 was the city's "heaviest building year in its history" (3, p. 35). Construction was valued at almost $24 million, including some $19 million for 563 single-family homes. The previous record had been $11 million for 503 homes in 1973.

Popular sentiment supporting growth control measures seemed enduring. As late as June 1986, a majority of voters supported advisory "Measure L," stating that Davis should grow as slowly as legally possible, and that annexations should be discouraged.

DEVELOPER CHALLENGES. As one might expect, progressive growth control was not popular with real estate developers (to use the mildest of characterizations). Yet they seemed by and large to accommodate to the situation. But not all. Several unsuccessful court challenges were made.

A new kind of challenge was mounted in 1986. Ramco Enterprises of West Sacramento approached the Yolo County Supervisors with a plan to develop 440 acres of residential, commercial, and industrial property outside the city on Davis's eastern border. After protracted struggle, the City Council agreed to annex the acreage and allow 105 new residences each year. Seeking to block this annexation and the project itself, a citizen-petition initiative was put on the 1989 ballot. Called "P" and "Q," both measures lost and the project proceeded (3; 4, ch. 6). (The official annexation in 1989—number 67—was 600 acres. In one stroke Davis increased from 7.5 to 8.5 square miles.)

Some observers chalked this conflict up as a victory for Frank Ramos (the apparent principal partner in Ramco Enterprises) specifically and developers more generally. Ramos had gone to the mat and got pretty much what he wanted. Although the Council won some battles in the form of land extractions and other features, it had, in some views, lost the war.

In this conflict, Ramos had successfully played the county supervisors against the Davis Council, forcing Davis to annex under the threat of county development. The Davis Council subsequently sought to forestall future such threats by what was called the "pass-through agreement." In this, the city purchased the county's promise not to develop on Davis borders with ongoing payments to the county from the city's redevelopment agency (cf. 2, December 31, 2001).

ENERGY CONSERVATION. Four 1970s social changes set the stage for Davis becoming an energy conservation pioneer. First, in a sudden burst of both fear and enthusiasm, U.S. environmental consciousness and action mushroomed in 1970 (e.g. "Earth Day" blossomed) and was high for some years. Second, this new consciousness was especially strong in Davis in part because of changes at UC Davis. In the 1960s, its College of Agriculture (and agricultural studies more generally) started to decline. This led to rethinking rationales and aims. Fitting with broader changes, missions were expanded to include environmental topics. The new 1967 name of the college signaled this: The College of Agricultural and Environmental Sciences. The idea of "ecology" began to take hold as "the catchword for a more holistic approach" to agriculture (24, p. 117).

Third, these two changes drew a new generation of environmentally concerned students to UC Davis, an influx that fit well with the environmentally conscious City Council. (Kopper, Tomasi, Black, and Evans, among other Davis activists, were UCD graduates imbued with this consciousness.) Fourth, there was a real energy crisis in the United States in 1973.

These four changes provided the context for creating and adopting innovative energy policies in Davis. These included the Energy Conservation Building Ordinance of 1975, which required the north-south orientation of all new construction and encouraged solar heating devices. This measure alone prompted some people to call Davis "Solar City" (3, p. 34). A city booklet describing the plan declared it "the first energy conservation building code in the country" (quoted in 4, ch. 2, p. 9). Along other lines, in October 1979, the Council approved an ordinance requiring that up to $500 be spent on retrofitted energy conservation measures as a condition of selling an existing home. When it went into effect on January 1, 1980, Davis became the first city in the nation to implement mandatory home energy conservation.

At the more general level of philosophy and approach, the 1973 General Plan itself was hailed as "a sophisticated, comprehensive energy conservation framework that called for a better integrated transportation system, innovative building regulations and public education" (4, ch. 2, p. 9). In October 1975, the Davis director of planning declared that the plan had "changed the shape of the city from sprawling suburbia to a well-managed, compact community" (quoted in 4, ch 2, p. 9).

VILLAGE HOMES. In his 2003 book, *Village Homes*, landscape architect Mark Francis writes that Davis had by that year become "a kind of environmental Mecca for foreign architects and planners who learn about it from television documentaries and books on ecological communities." As an internationally renowned expert on these topics, Professor Francis was frequently asked to give tours of Davis to visiting groups of these professionals.

He reports, "it is always interesting to see their reaction when they arrive in Davis. A typical reaction is to look a bit confused by the more standard layout of the community." Cynics would say that these visitors are properly bewildered because there is in fact little in Davis that is not common elsewhere. But Professor Francis opines that the problem is that the "innovation is hidden."

Be that as it may, foreign visitors are not confused by the 60-acre, 244-home residential area in far west Davis called Village Homes. They may be disappointed with how most of Davis looks, but not by that neighborhood. It was often described as constituted of "lush and extensive open spaces." According to Francis, visitors commonly comment, "this would be a great place to live."

By all accounts, such sentiments are not confined to visiting planners. Celebrity Americans such as Rosalynn Carter, Jane Fonda, and Pete Seeger have made their own treks to Village Homes. And the place seems equally or more popular with the people who actually live there.

Such acclaim and reverence was not always so. Indeed, the Village Homes story is the classic one we know and love and that we have already heard regarding bicycles: the triumph of vision, goodness and persistence over narrow-mindedness, risk-aversion, and bureaucratic rigidity.

The visionaries in this case were Judy and Mike Corbett, in their early 30s in 1972. They reported their situation:

> We had no financial assets and no track record in development. We were embarking on a large-scale project that incorporated numerous untried and innovative features. . . . [But,] luck was on our side. It took a great deal of tenacity and perseverance, but in the end we were able to overcome multiple obstacles and build Village Homes (quoted in 5, p. 20).

The obstacles included the Davis director of planning laughing at Mike when he first presented the development map to her. She told him to come back when he met the building code. FHA officials, whose approval for insuring mortgages was critical, disliked a long list of the plan's features, which included narrow, winding streets and extensive solar installations in each home.

Over time, though, the energy conservation ferment then percolating in Davis began to soften the views of city officials. But it was the Davis City Council that finally saved the project. The Corbetts appealed negative lower decisions to the council and, in the words of Judy Corbett, "the City Council was very liberal and supportive of what we were doing." Mark Francis reports, "After almost three years of delays and negotiations, they were allowed to begin construction of the first houses in 1975" (5, p. 30).

So began what would become a distinctive feature of Davis, a town that otherwise looked much like an Orange County "slurb." Innovative features of what wags called "Corbettville" included its explicit effort to "recreate a traditional sense of community and to conserve energy and water. . . . Solar water heating and passive space heating [were] . . . incorporated into the design of each home" (Davis Conference and Visitors Bureau website text, 2004).

DOWNTOWN DEVELOPMENT. Although a clear commitment to Davis having a downtown was made in the "exploding" period, the going was not easy over the 1970s and 1980s. The lack of large parcels made it difficult to site a large store. Further, Davisites were ambivalent about large stores anyway, especially those that were units of national chains. Moreover, Davis's very (albeit limited) success in slowing its growth made it of marginal interest to large store builders because its population was so small.

These attitudes and limitations were clearly displayed in the protracted problem of developing the block bounded by Third, B, Fourth, and C. It had become vacant in 1966 and would remain so until its dedication as an extension of Central Park in 1990—a period of 34 years. Early on, the block was going to have an Arden-Mayfair grocery store. That project never started, but people began to call the block "Arden-Mayfair" anyway. In 1985, it was leased to Terranomics to build a two-level shopping center with some two dozen retail stores and 300 parking places, among other features.

One might think this was exactly the kind of thing one needed for a developed downtown; but no, a citizen initiative put the project to a vote in June 1986 and defeated it. This happened in part because the decision was framed as a park versus a shopping center. A "yes" vote made the block an extension of Central Park, which meant no shopping center. "Yes" got 60 percent of the vote. With that, Fourth Street between B and C was eliminated and Central Park more than doubled in size. Of some import, a covered plaza for the Farmers' Market was subsequently built along C just north of Third. Other amenities were added.

Led by Mayor Bill Kopper, efforts at "adaptive reuse" of older buildings rather than demolition began in the early 1970s. Almost a dozen of such projects were completed by the late 1980s, including Orange Court at 125–137 E and Park Place at 216–228 D. These and other reconfigurations of older buildings greatly contributed to the sense that Davis still had a traditional downtown.

Expanding the time-frame to include the next period, the City of Davis became a major historic preservation/rehabilitation presence in the downtown over the 1970 to the 1990s. Lurching from situation to situation, it became the owner or controller of: the old Davis High School remodeled into a city hall (late 1970s); the Southern Pacific Rail station (1980s); the old library remodeled into a meeting room/museum (1980s–1990s); the Dresbach-Hunt-Boyer Mansion (1994); the long-term lease on and remodel of the Varsity Theater (1990s); the old city hall (for decades the only building the city owned); and the Boy Scout Cabin, on which the city had a lease with an option to buy the land from UC Davis, giving it operational if not actual ownership (14, p. 110). (More than a decade into the contested period, stewardship of the Dresbach-Hunt-Boyer Mansion, the Varsity Theater, the old city hall, and the Boy Scout Cabin would prove to be highly problematic.)

THE COUNCIL'S FOREIGN POLICIES. Continuing a longstanding practice of adopting policies on matters outside its jurisdiction (e.g. banning Japanese nationals in California), the Council took stands on these among other matters: *1972*, supported the Equal Rights Amendment; *1982*, supported a bilateral freeze on production of nuclear weapons (3–2 vote); *1986*, declared Davis a sanctuary city; *1989*, declared Davis a "Pro-Choice" city (3–0 with two abstentions); *1989* (signaling the near-end of the era), voted down a proposed nuclear-free ordinance. (Interest in the pro-choice question ran so high that the meeting on it was held before an overflowing crowd in the largest room of the Veterans Memorial.)

FAULTERING CITY AND UC DAVIS FINANCING. One of the roots of the expansiveness of the Davis government in the earlier 1970s was a strong economy and burgeoning property taxes. Things soon changed.

Proposition 13 Staggered Local Government. On June 6, 1978, the California electorate adopted the famous "Proposition 13," which limited increases in property taxes. Yolo County was one of the few areas that voted against it and this was due to the heavy negative vote in Davis. Across the state, local governments were forced to lay off employees. Davis laid off 23 and the Davis-area school district laid off 28. At the Council meeting of June 21, 1978, two members voted (perhaps in jest) to "stop supplying pens and pencils to . . . City employees." The motion failed with two members against and one absent.

Rough Times But Growth at UC Davis. In the previous chapter I described Louis Menand's analysis of 1945–1975 as the golden era of the American college. Around 1975, higher education began to stall. "The student deferment was abolished and American involvement in the war ended; the college-age population stopped growing; the country went into recession; and the economic value of a college degree began to fall. . . . A system that had quintupled . . . in the span of a generation suddenly found itself with empty dormitory beds and a huge tenured faculty (18, p. 47).

UC Davis was equally hit. I was a professor of sociology there at this time and I remember serious discussions of how UC might not need a department for every subject on every campus. Why not, for example, geography on three campuses rather than on eight or nine of them? Redundancy lay-offs of tenured professors loomed, raising the question of whether one's tenure was in UC as a whole or only at Davis. No one was certain. Every expenditure was up for review, right down to removing almost all the telephones. In February 1982, a major campus concern was that budget cuts would result in the loss of about 2,300 students and over a hundred faculty.

Somehow, UC Davis survived and even did rather well. Despite all the agony and financial and staff soul searching, the campus had almost twice as many students in 1990 (22,000) as it had in 1970 (12,600).

PUBLIC CRISIS AND DRAMA. In the sweep of Davis history, the progressive period likely stands above the other eight in the number and intensity of its dramatic political events. By "dramatic political events" I mean occasions on which large numbers of emotionally aroused people assembled to demand that officials act or not act, acts of nonviolent protest took place, and/or an atmosphere of crisis prevailed. A number of these have been mentioned in connection with other matters already described in this chapter. Let me record just one more: the iconic—albeit brief—transportation stoppage of May 9, 1972. Responding to Nixon's resumption of North

Vietnam bombing, "several hundred Davisites spread out on Interstate 80, briefly blocking the freeway. Later the same day about 60 people sat on and blocked the railroad tracks near the SP station." Council member Bob Black was among those arrested (3, p. 33).

DAVIS BECAME A CELEBRITY. Like people, places can be celebrities. One way this happens is that people who are celebrities say, "this place is a celebrity." It is an anointing process in which existing celebrities make new ones. Further, once the process is started, other celebrities join in and bask in the new light. And then, the celebrity machine—the mass media—fuels and amplifies cycles of celebration.

Something of this sort appears to have happened to Davis in the later 1970s. The kickoff celebrity-making event was First Lady Rosalynn Carter's visit in March 1979. She toured Village Homes, rode on a London double-decker bus, pedaled a bicycle on a greenbelt, and had dinner with selected members of the progressive elite at the home of Mayor Tom Tomasi. She also attended a special meeting of the City Council where she presented leaders with honors for energy conservation (3, p. 36).

A news account of this visit described a moment on the bus tour when Mrs. Carter remarked to Council members Bill Kopper and Tom Tomasi and solar designer Marshall Hunt: " 'Y'all are so young,' . . . amid laughter" (2, March 21, 1979). And so they were. Mrs. Carter had seen a significant feature of the Davis progressive era that was often overlooked. Environmental concern, growth control, and other flourishing policies in Davis were very much "children's crusades." Major movers such as Bob Black and Bill Kopper were baby boomers, cohorts of the baby-boomer-in-chief, President Bill Clinton.

Four months after Mrs. Carter's visit, her husband, President Jimmy Carter, made a major address to the nation on energy in which he praised Davis for doing a "tremendous job" in reducing its use. This was heavy celebrity anointing. It kicked the celebrity machine into high gear. Magazines, newspapers, and televisions stations around the world did features on Davis. Some of them even bothered to go there and poke around.

After the initial burst, celebrity simmered. U.S. Secretary of Energy Charles Duncan visited in January 1980. Actress Jane Fonda chose a Davis theater for the July 1982 northern California premier of her *On Golden Pond*. In March 1984, French president Francois Mitterrand visited Davis in order to see Village Homes (landing there in a helicopter). (Apocryphal reports had it that Mitterand thought all of Davis looked like Village Homes and that the city resembled a typical French village.)

* * *

In the 1970s and 1980s Davis became, in the inspired phrase of Bob Dunning quoted previously, "The City of All Things Right and Relevant." But like previous periods, this one was a passing phase rather than an enduring trait.

Chapter Nine

CONTESTED DAVIS, 1990–

Although the year 1990 was not as dramatic or profound as years like 1945 and 1972, reflective people observing Davis that year nonetheless saw it as a turning point. In retrospect, it was.

Only four candidates stood for the two open seats on the City Council that year. Two, Susie Boyd and Lois Wolk, described themselves as moderates. They meant this as a contrast to progressives. The position of the third was unclear. The fourth was the incumbent and progressive mayor, the famous maverick developer Mike Corbett. Former mayor Ann Evans, a progresssive, had decided not to seek a third term. Progressives did not field another of their own to run with Corbett for the other open seat.

Corbett drew 40 percent of the votes, but was short of the winning 44 percent received by Boyd and far behind Wolk's 58 percent (one of the highest seen in many elections before and after 1990).

Wolk and Boyd positioned themselves to the center-right of Corbett. A panel of ex-mayors conversing on Davis Community Television the evening of this election day agreed that these two had forged a new, winning posture. Bob Black, Bill Kopper, Dave Rosenberg, and Jim Stevens opined the end of an era. Echoing this, the *Enterprise* year-end summary of 1990 characterized the election as "a significant turning point in Davis politics. . . . [The balance of power on the council has shifted away] "from progressives for the first time in almost 20 years" (2, December 31, 1990).

POLITICAL CONTESTS. Like the progressives before them, moderate power was precarious. Indeed, the idea of "contest" in the sense of engagements with uncertain outcomes appropriately labeled at least the first dozen or so years after 1990.

In the nine city council elections between 1990 and 2004, the top vote-receivers—and therefore mayors—were moderate five times and progressive four times. As seen in the "Progressive-Moderate Split" category in the table below, all but one of eight councils had moderate majorities. Further, among the 40 Council positions between 1990 and 2004, moderates held 26 and progressives only 14. The term "contest" might characterize this period, but the contestants had not, so far, faired equally at the ballot box. (See the table on the following page.)

Years	Lowest Winning %	Highest %	Progressive-Moderate Split	Mayor
1990–1992	44	58	1/4	Moderate (Skinner)
1992–1994	39	43	2/3	Moderate (Wolk)
1994–1996	29	43	2/3	Progressive (Rosenberg)
1996–1998	33	39	1/4	Moderate (Wolk)
1998–2000	38	43	2/3	Progressive (Partansky)
2000–2002	31	43	3/2	Progressive (Wagstaff)
2002–2004	53	54	2/3	Moderate (Boyd)
2004–2006	36	39	1/4	Moderate (R. Asmundson)
2006–2008	scheduled based on 2004 election: Progressive (Greenwald)			

As reported in previous chapters, the percentage of votes needed to win a council seat declined over the urbanizing, depression, exploding, and progressive periods. This erosion continued and got to the point of electing someone with 29 percent (13, p. 9). Also, the percentages began to level off. As seen above, the lowest-winning percents averaged in the high 30s, while 39 and 43 were often the highest percentages, making their recipients the mayor.

In the later years of the progressive period, the conventional wisdom in the Davis "political class" (the few hundred people who watched its politics closely) was that voters divided into one-third each progressives, moderates, and the middling-uncertains. Winning an election therefore required getting 5–10 or so percent more than one's base third. Because only progressives or moderates had ideologies articulate enough to prompt serious campaigns, the central task was to draw support from the middling-uncertains.

But this picture of one-third each was problematic and increasingly so as the years went on. Despite the stereotype of being anti-growth, Davis was in fact growing quite substantially. (Over 1993–2003, "no growth" Davis grew 28 percent, as compared to 21 percent and 20 percent for "pro growth" Woodland and West Sacramento, and 22 percent for Yolo County [*Sacramento Bee*, April 21, 2004].) Moreover, the growth was heavily in far east and south Davis, places with expensive housing developments. Therefore, one might expect the percent of moderates to increase.

There was some evidence of this shift, but also contrary signs. In the 2004 election, for example, the two candidates who ran most clearly on their ideological bases—progressive Mike Harrington and moderate Donna Lott— received votes suggesting that each still had about one-third of the electorate. Both got 33 percent.

Stability was also suggested by the fact that Davis continued to vote heavily Democratic in wider elections. Indeed, the extraordinary governor's recall election of October 7, 2003, offered vivid evidence of a still strong leftward tilt. These were the results for Davis, the State of California, and San Francisco:

	Davis	California	San Francisco
Percent "Yes," recall Gray Davis:	44	55	20
Percent Voting for:			
Camajo (Green)	9	3	6
Bustamante (Democrat)	46	32	63
Schwarzenegger (Republican)	28	49	19
McClintock (Conservative Republican)	8	13	6

Grey Davis survived the recall vote in only a small minority of California jurisdictions. But he was retained by 56 percent in Davis. On the question of a new governor, 55 percent favored a candidate of the left, as compared to 35 percent who felt that way statewide. As the above figures also show, Davis was not as left as San Francisco, the state's most liberal jurisdiction. Nonetheless, it was also clearly to the left of California as a whole.

GROWTH DEBATES. Growth as an issue defined the 1972 start of the progressive era. In one or another guise or venue, it continued as the central debate in civic life. If anything, disputes over it became more intense as the years went on. Among many of these disputes between 1990 and the early zero years of the twenty-first century, eight involved particularly large growth plans or were otherwise noteworthy.

(1) In the same 1990 election that brought moderates to power, voters rejected citizen initiative Measure C that would have limited Davis growth to 1.78 percent per year. "A late campaign, financed up front by Councilman Maynard Skinner, helped contribute to an overwhelming vote . . . [against it]. Skinner later paid off the campaign debt with a fund-raiser attended by builders, real estate interest and area developers" (2, December 31, 1990). (2) A 44-acre "Gateway project" west of Olive Drive between I-80 and the railroad and containing major retail dominated late 1993 news and the election campaign of 1994. Given a negative reception for, among other reasons, claims of likely harm to the Downtown, a revision with much less retail was still criticized. The developers dropped the proposal.

(3) The "Wildhorse project" to build a golf course and about 800 housing units in northeast Davis was disputed some seven years before final approval in 1995. That year, the project was put to a citizen referendum that would have voided the development agreement the Council had approved (on a split vote). Voters "overwhelmingly turned down the referendum" (2, December 31, 1995). (4) Also in the mid-1990s, developer John Whitcombe sought to launch "Covell Center" on almost 400 acres at the northwest corner of Covell and Pole Line. To sweeten the deal, he offered to build and donate to the city a 75-acre "sports complex." This attraction mobilized a Davis Sports Coalition, but it was not enough to overcome fears that the complex would be a Trojan Horse. The city's dire financial situation meant it likely could not afford to

operate and maintain such a facility. The project died (but rose from the dead, as we see below).

(5) Starting in the late progressive period, City Councils decided to allow new housing to be built faster than originally scheduled—a process called "front loading." One consequence was a down-turn in housing production at the turn of the millenium. This new "squeeze" provided a reason for a moderate Council majority to begin to authorize, in September 2002, 250 housing units a year more than allowed by the General Plan. Because Davis had already met its regional fair-share housing obligation through 2006, progressives decried this as runaway growth. (6) In March 2000, 54 percent of voters approved a Council-proposed measure requiring a "vote of the people if the City Council approves development on land outside of city limits" (2, December 31, 2000). Identified as "J" on the ballot, the phrase "Measure J vote" became an active element of Davis political talk. (As of the publication of this book, the council had yet seriously to review and decide on a project requiring a Measure J vote.)

(7) In November 2000, 70 percent of voters approved Measure O, which taxed residents $24 a year for 30 years "to pay for the purchase of open space around the city's borders" (2, December 31, 2000). The measure created a citizens' commission to recommend purchases and it reported in early 2004. The moderate-dominated council rejected the commission's proposals for purchases close to Davis's borders and opted for more distant parcels. This caused turmoil among the commissioners and residents more widely, many of whom denounced the action as violating what they believed was the clear intent of the measure. (8) The Covell Commons proposal died, but the desire to develop the land did not. The owners offered a new plan in 2003, this time containing 1,400 units of housing under the new name "Covell Village" (an especially cynical new name, progressive opponents thought).

Expressing the idea of a "contested" Davis, these eight growth debates (and others not reported here) could be characterized by moderates and progressives alike as "you win some, you lose some."

A CONSENSUS EXCEPTION: THE DOWNTOWN. We have seen that the Downtown assumed a special and affectionate status in Davis life early in the exploding period and that this continued through the progressive era. In what might be regarded as an amazing phenomenon of political consensus, this status continued into the twenty-first century. Virtually to a person, candidates for City Council subscribed to the idea of keeping the downtown the center of Davis. Indeed, one of the few candidates who questioned this doctrine—thrice-elected Jerry Adler—was defeated in his 1996 run for a fourth term. He declared, "We cannot foster the myth that . . . [the Downtown] is the retail center . . . The County Fair Mall in Woodland is the retail center of Davis" (2, December 31, 1996). In this sense, the downtown was a sacred cow.

Myriad actions especially helpful to the Downtown were policies and programs or signal events and episodes.

Policies and programs were active in four main areas. (a) Although the Davis Redevelopment Agency (RDA) was created in the early 1970s, a project area was not defined until the late 1980s. The one created contained South Davis, Olive Drive, and the Downtown. Financed largely by tax increment accruals, about $30 million was spent (or budgeted for spending) to reduce "blight" in the Downtown over the 1990–2005 period. This was about half of all RDA expenditures and budget commitments for those years. Downtown "blight" reduction activities and plans included street realignment and circulation improvement, corner crosswalk beautification, general amenity enhancements (e.g. facade improvement loans), and fee-forgiveness for construction projects. Perhaps most dramatically, $5 million was used to redevelop the entire block at the southeast corner of Fifth and G.

(b) Historically, the Chamber of Commerce was the voice of Davis business, but this ended in the later 1980s as downtown businesses developed a distinctive consciousness. In 1988, this consciousness achieved organizational form as the Davis Downtown Business Association (DDBA). A non-profit corporation, it was also a city-sanctioned business improvement district (a "BID"). As a quasi-official extension of the city government, the city administered an assessment that supported it. In 2003, 700 or so businesses generated close to $100,000 for it (over half of the total DDBA budget). A National Trust "Main Street Community" since 2000, the DDBA was directed by an elected board and the array of committees required by that program. Coordinated by an executive director and staff, the organization carried on a year-round schedule of promotional events, downtown maintenance, lobbying the city government, and other activities.

(c) On the city side, in addition to the ordinary services provided by over 400 city employees, most or a good part of the time of five of the upper-level staff were spent on programs specific to helping the Downtown. (d) Later in this period, the city developed three bodies of Downtown policy containing many rules for managing the area: *The Core Area Specific Plan*, 1996; the *Core Area Strategy Report & Five-Year Action Plan*, 2000, and *the Davis Downtown and Traditional Residential Neighborhood Design Guidelines*, 2001. These documents were informed by a Jane Jacobs/new urbanism vision. Among more important specific policies was the idea that only retail should be in ground-level locations, that offices and services should be above ground level, and that residences should be provided on second and higher levels of buildings. Led by developer Chuck Roe, several downtown buildings constructed after 1996 exhibited this pattern.

A number of episodes and events affected the Downtown and arguably helped it. (a) The auto tunnel under the railroad track that entered the downtown at First and E was a recurring concern. Plans to widen it had been put before the electorate in 1968, 1973, 1987, and 1997, and failed each time. Reasons for failure varied, but the 1997 struggle was (among other things) a moderate-progressive conflict over visions of the Downtown and, by extension, Davis. Moderates sought "an open invitation for people . . . to swerve off I-80 and come into our wonderful town" (councilmember Jerry

Kaneko, 2, December 31, 1996). This was a vision of "Davis As Carmel." But the specter of a freeway-wide boulevard dumping thousands of cars an hour into the Downtown horrified progressives such as Mayor Julie Partansky and fellow participants in SMART (Save Money and Reduce Traffic). For opponents, widening would destroy the town's "old-fashioned, pedestrian-friendly . . . small town character" (4, ch. 8, p. 1). The widening was rejected by a vote of 56 percent.

(b) Also in 1997, a small mall called "Davis Commons" was proposed for the southwest corner of First Street and the Richards Underpass. It would contain a Borders bookstore, a fact that galvanized progressive defenders of small retailers, especially independent bookstores. Despite campaigning and a lawsuit, the Commons, with a Borders, opened in September of 1998. (c) After more than a decade of relatively little construction in the Downtown, there was a spate of new—often three and four story—buildings and other projects in the later 1990s and early 2000s. These included the Fifth and G Streets US Department of Agriculture building, theaters, and parking structure; Davis Commons; the E Street Plaza; the Natsoulas Gallery; the Lofts (see the picture on page 100); the Chen Building; and the McCormick building. A DDBA official estimated that in 1999–2003, combined pubic-private capital investments were over $60 million.

DOWN AND UP AT UCD. People long involved with UCD sometimes compared the experience to riding a roller coaster. Thrilling ascents and highs alternated with terrifying dives and lows. We saw this in previous periods and it happened again in this period. But also as previously, the longer-term trend remained large growth and ever-greater academic and other strengths.

The 1990s opened with severe budget cuts. Among other curtailments, the UC retirement system surplus was used to induce one-quarter of the *entire* (not just senior) faculty to retire in 1991–1994.

The economic bubble of the later 1990s fueled UC's comeback. And another turn of history protected it somewhat from the larger economic bust of the early 2000s. This historical turn was the children of the baby-boomers reaching college age. Labeled "tidal wave II," this cohort started to enter college in the early 2000s. If UC was to continue to meet its founding commitment to admit the top one-eighth of graduating high school seniors, it had to expand its capacities in a major way.

The UC Regents assigned UCD a middling portion of the total growth necessary. In the year 2001, the UCD on-campus daily population was about 36,000 (24,000 students, 11,000 faculty and staff, and 1,000 other workers). The UC Regents told UCD planners that by 2016 the daily on-campus population should be about 52,000 (30,000 students, 15,000 faculty and staff, and 7,000 other workers, who would be heavily associated with a new research park and a neighborhood educational center). This was an increase of 16,000 people over 15 years, a rate and scale of growth not seen at UCD since the boom of the 1960s. (Figures rounded from the April 2003 *UCD Long Range Development Plan*, p. 5).

It was a massive planning task and made especially problematic because Davis had adopted Measure J. From UCD's point of view, Davis was, in effect, a no-growth city. How could one add 16,000 people to a no-growth city?

Among several strategies, two were quite public. First, it created a new unit to organize the growth, one that reported directly to the chancellor. In a stroke of strategic genius, it hired Davis City Manager John Meyer to head that unit. Meyer was a UCD graduate and a municipal government boy wonder. He had become Davis city manager in 1990 at age 33, the youngest in California. A success in that job, he was famous for the relaxed and humor-laced manner in which he could get people to work hard and together—qualities UCD would need a lot of in the years to come. Previously employed at UCD as an undergraduate assistant in the library, his May 2000 UCD appointment was as the Vice Chancellor for Resource Management and Planning.

Second, the UCD campus was in the auspicious situation of owning thousands of acres of open land that stretched for miles to the west and south of the main campus. Created as an independent entity in the California constitution, UC (and therefore UCD) was functionally sovereign. No local government had to approve its plans for construction and development. It had its own municipal and social infrastructure: electricity grid, sewer system, water wells, custodial and public works workers, groundskeepers/parks department, mail distribution system, police force, and fire department.

It was a de facto municipality and bureaucratically organized as a quasi-socialist state. There was little to inhibit it envisioning and planning an entirely new neighbored/community on the open fields at the southwest corner of Russell and 113. And this it did.

The process of public review UCD elected to provide involved many meetings with residents, some of which elicited strong negative reactions. People living directly north of the proposed neighborhood were especially alarmed by the prospect of thousands of new vehicles on Russell Boulevard. In an effort at compromise, UCD cut the planned population and eliminated vehicular connection to Russell. When approved by the UC Regents in November 2003, the build-out population was set at 4,300, down from an initial 6,200 (2, December 31, 2003).

Massive growth was not the only UCD fact or aspiration. Having started as "The Farm" that catered to rural folk, the campus has long carried the stigma of the "backward hick." Increasingly, UCD leaders wanted to transcend this past by "reintroducing" the campus to the public. Two elements of the strategy they devised were calculated to be highly visible locally and to bring national visibility. First, new resources were invested in the arts and, in particular, in constructing a world-class concert hall in which the best artists could perform and in which the most important leaders of all kinds could appear.

Second, this (and other) "reintroducing" structures would be located at a new UCD "front door." The front door of the original campus was on the state highway (named Russell Boulevard). When Route 40 and then I-80 bypassed Davis, it became obsolete. However, considerable open land lay between the Putah Creek channel and the Interstate 80 freeway passing south of the main campus. Highly visible from I-80, this area was planned as a new campus center consisting of a number of "welcoming structures" at this "front door." By 2003, two of the four sides of a new "quad" had been occupied: the Buehler Alumni and Visitors Center and the Mondavi Center for the Performing Arts. Yet to come was a hotel and conference center on the east side and a major art gallery to the south. (A large parking garage at the southwest corner had already been completed.)

Not everything was blissful at burgeoning UCD. Spurred by the war on terrorism, in the early 2000s the federal government began funding new laboratories for research on dangerous biological entities. Some would work with the most deadly of entities and were, in the lingo, "Level Four" labs. UCD leaders decided to apply for one. The application proposed to put it at the northeast corner of the intersection of two freeways, Interstate 80 and Route 113 (only a few hundred yards west of the new "front door").

In January 2003, UCD officials publicly presented the proposal to the Davis City Council and asked for its endorsement. This was only a short time before the government's deadline. Because of this, the immediate and strong public outcry contained both procedural and substantive objections. Critics thought UCD officials were arrogant and in bad faith to propose something so dangerous with virtually no time for public review nor any opportunity to consider alternative locations. Substantively, situating the most dangerous organisms in the world at the intersection of two freeways was, some said, bizarre (aside from its proximity to a population soon to approach 100,000). The projected building would be a conspicuous four stories with a large footprint. Its visibility from both I-80 and 113 would surely invite drive-by terrorist attacks. Amidst several heated public meetings, the Davis City Council voted unanimously to ask UCD not to site the lab in Davis. Seemingly unperturbed, UCD went forth with the application, unaltered. It was turned down in September 2003.

Prior to the biolab brouhaha, most Davisites tended to assume that, for the most part, UCD officials could be trusted to do the right thing and to act reasonably. Combined with other worrisome actions—such as a Downtown-harmful plan for a hotel and conference center—the biolab prompted some people to question that assumption. Such reckless and imperious behavior raised the possibility, in the views of many, that something was seriously awry in the upper levels of the UCD hierarchy.

FROM ECO-CITY TO WEIRD DAVIS. Recall that Davis became a celebrity in the late 1970s and early 1980s when First Lady Rosalynn Carter and French president Francois Mitterrand visited to inspect pioneering energy measures. This celebrity status had two features. First, Davis was characterized as a serious place that did positive things. It was a hero. Second, over the 1980s and the early 1990s, this status faded. By the early 1990s, Davis was receiving little media attention.

But then something odd happened. In 1993, the media spotlight shone on Davis again. However, this time it was negative. Instead of being a hero, the town was treated as a weird and quirky fool. Other negative labels included goofy, odd, eccentric, and flaky (2, September 29, 1994; 4, Ch. 10). One way to understand this change is as a media-fueled process that knitted together four distorted events spaced over about two years.

The precipitating incident was the Council's passing of a no-smoking law on February 17, 1993. In Davis, this was hardly a story at all. But because of media response to it, the *Enterprise* elevated it to sixth in its list of top ten 1993 stories. "Davis garners worldwide attention again, this time for one of the toughest anti-smoking laws in the nation" (2, December 31, 1993).

Eleven months later, in January 1994, a person complained to the police that he was kept awake by snoring sounds coming through his bedroom wall from the adjoining duplex. The noise abatement officer confirmed that the noise rose to offending levels and cited the snorer. National media had a field day. The incident was number one on the *Enterprise*'s list of top ten 1994 stories.

In June of this same year, Davis resident Charles Goldman appeared before the City Council to express his concern about the survival of the thousands of toads that lived beside a Pole Line Road site where a freeway overpass was about to be built. The overpass would disrupt the migratory path of the toads and thereby wipe them out. However, the problem could be solved by installing a tunnel under the overpass through which the toads could migrate, a solution, he said, that was successful in other places. Members of the Council liked the idea and the additional cost was authorized. Writing about this, Bob Dunning opined, "It's an idea whose time has come. It's Davis. Yes, it's Davis" (2, June 22, 1994). This event is reported to have drawn modest media attention (4). But it did not make the *Enterprise*'s 1994 year-end round up of top ten stories (even in the "also happened" category).

Last, but certainly not least, in February 1995, a *Sacramento Bee* reporter interviewed councilmember Julie Partansky on the then-issue of paving or leaving as gravel six alleys in an early twentieth-century neighborhood just north of the Downtown. Partansky was familiar with historic preservation concepts and law, but the reporter was not. Partansky suggested that gravel alleys might be considered a feature of the Old North—a historic neighborhood—and therefore kept gravel (a view that was, in 2001, adopted into Davis conservation district law applying to the Old North). However, as *Enterprise* reporter Howard Beck observed, what the reporter heard and passed on to other media was like the kid's game "operator." "A message is whispered from one ear to the next, and by the time it comes out the other end, the original message has . . . become a humorous parody of itself"(2, March 10, 1995). In this case, "gravel alleys plus historical [preservation] issues plus pot holes in the possibly historic alleys equals 'historic potholes'" (2, March 10, 1995). Without checking, CBS radio and other media claimed that Partansky had said that federal law "requires the potholes be left unfilled" (2, March 10, 1995).

Beck also made the important point that, by February 1995, Davis had become "a frequent source of oddball news," namely the smoking, snoring, and toad tunnel stories of the previous two years. As merely "more of the same," distant reporters did not feel they had to check on the pothole story's authenticity (which they did not). Anything was likely true in that strange town.

And so there it was: Weird Davis. The reality of each of these stories was, of course, distorted by the media. Like all stereotypes, once set in motion they were, as a practical matter, impossible to rebut or shake.

But perhaps there was more to this than selective perception built on the accidents of four events. Recall that Davis's claims-to-fame in the 1960s and 1970s were the heroic "Bike City" and "Eco-City" images. A place that makes claims to high virtue may also be setting itself up to be seen as pretentious. Everybody remembers that kid in the sixth grade no one could stand because he or she always had a hand up eager to answer the teacher's questions, always with his or her homework done, and who aced every exam. Oh how delicious it was to see that kid make a mistake. Davis may have become that too-eager and too-smart kid. The events of 1993–1995 were payback time. Pompous (and affluent and educated) Davis was getting its comeuppance.

Viewed in wider perspective, a deep and old anti-intellectual narrative in American life may also have played out here: The smart-alec intellectual who claims high virtue and pioneering triumphs (in bikes, energy, or what have you) is unmasked as a bumbling fool.

QUESTS FOR DISTINCTIVE IDENTITY. Leaders of American communities have long tried to devise distinctive identities for their locales. They have wanted glowing answers to the questions, "What is our place about?" and "What is distinctive about our place?"

Historically, Davis leaders shared this quest. The Davis Arch spanning Second Street from 1916 to 1924 was an early and ambitious such effort. As seen in the picture on page 74, the arch read "Davis" in the middle and declared, on the left, "Gateway to Yolo County" and, on the right, "Home of University Farm." These were bold declarations of what the place was about and what was distinctive to it.

In the 1920s, prize-winning livestock farms encircled Davis. The abundance of first-place, purple ribbons garnered by these farms prompted Davis movers and shakers to label the area "The Purple Circle" (7, p. 23). As the center of the circle, Davis's identity was obvious.

My impression is that Davis came onto identity hard-times over the 1930s–1950s. Recall that in 1953 the Chamber of Commerce even held a contest intended to elicit an identity from the public, but the effort was unsuccessful (Ch. 7; 2, March 30, 1953). It was only in the late 1960s, and then almost by accident, that a "unique feature" of Davis was discovered or invented (depending on how you look at it). Joyously, Davis became "the bike capitol of the world" (see chapter 7).

Bike City was, though, a rather narrow identity. In the 1970s, events converged in a way to make it possible to incorporate bikes into the wider and more serious identity of energy use innovation and conservation. "Eco-City" (as in ecological) took its place alongside or even above "Bike City."

Identities seem prone to fade. Factors that cause this likely include loss of freshness and resonance; weakening of the reality that fostered them initially; and adoption by the larger society so that they become unremarkably commonplace.

Whatever the reasons, Davis identities devised before World War II have long since lapsed. Moreover, the Bike City image born in the 1960s and the

Eco-City image arising in the 1970s seemed in the process of fading in the 1990s and later. Regarding Bike City, several studies and everyday observation showed a marked decline in bike use over the 1990s and into the 2000s. "Bike culture" among the shrinking number of riders also receded in such ways as obedience to rules of the road and assignment of officers to enforce bike laws. Decline in bike use among high school students was especially dramatic (as was increase in SUV use among them).

It is sometimes said that "nothing fails like success" and such appeared the fate of Davis as Eco-City and leadership in energy conservation. Solar and energy standards and practices spread and developed further after the 1980s, but Davis stalled. This was because, in Mike Fitch's view, political "leaders had to spend much of their energy fixing financial and other problems, and were less inclined to launch ambitious initiatives" (4, Introduction, p. 3). But hope, at least, continued. In 2004, the chair of a Citizen Task Force on Energy Issues declared to the City Council that "Davis has been a leader [in energy matters] . . . and we can be a leader again."

It might be said then that, by the later 1990s, Davis was once again "identity-challenged." One response was to "whistle past the graveyard," as shown in the picture on page 99. A second was to embrace and make positive the negative identity of Weird Davis (a response sometimes adopted by stigmatized groups, as in inverting the meaning of the word queer). In 1999, resident Ted Puntillo self-published a colorfully illustrated children's book titled *The Toads of Davis*. It celebrated the toad tunnel and saving the toads, and sold thousands of copies locally. This stimulated increasingly wide use of the toad as a Davis symbol—and perhaps the identity of Weird Davis. In 2004, the city even acquired a custom-constructed toad costume, seen on page 99, for a hapless volunteer to suffocate in at a May "Celebrate Davis" day in Community Park (meaning "sell-a-brate" by shopping in town). Staged close to the city's iconic but decades-broken Solar Panel Structure, this was a vivid juxtaposition of fading and brightening identities.

* * *

This history of Davis has featured the themes "radical changes, deep constants." The radical changes have been obvious, especially as regards increases in population and territory and the social changes accompanying them.

Among deep constants, let me close by calling attention to one that has especially engaged me. From the first issue of the *Davis Advertiser* in 1869 down to the most recent *Davis Enterprise*, public figures have portrayed Davis as a special place of promise with uniquely positive attractions. While such civic boosterism is seen in virtually all communities, the Davis version seems particularly exercised, energetic, and eager. Any number of programs and policies launched over some 14 decades have earnestly sought to give reality to boosteristic proclamations.

The cumulative consequence is a kind of super-achiever, "gee whiz" ethos that hints of desperation and trying too hard. But even though the facts may sometimes fall short of the claims, the rhetoric of specialness remains compelling.

REFERENCES

In the text, a reference is identified by its number in this list.

1. *Davisville Advertiser.* December 1869–May 1870. (Microfilm, University Library, University of California, Davis).
2. *Davis Enterprise.* 1898 to date. Davis, CA: *The Davis Enterprise.*
3. Diemer, William D. 2000. ed. *Davis From the Inside Out, A Municipal Almanac, Volume 1: Davis as City.* Davis, CA: National Housing Register.
4. Fitch, Mike. 1998. *Growing Pains: Thirty Years in the History of Davis.* Davis: The City of Davis Website (www.city.davis.ca.us/pb/cultural/about.cfm).
5. Francis, Mark. 2003. *Village Homes: A Community By Design.* Washington, DC: Island Press.
6. Kelley, Robert. 1989. *Battling the Inland Sea: Floods, Public Policy, and the Sacramento Valley.* Berkeley, CA: University of California Press.
7. Larkey, Joann Leach. 1969. *Davisville '68: The History and Heritage of the City of Davis, Yolo County, California.* Davis, CA: The Davis Historical and Landmarks Commission.
8. ———. 1969–1973. *The Larkey Articles: One-Hundred and Sixty Four "Portraits of the Past" Articles Published by Joann Leach Larkey in the Davis Enterprise Between December 4, 1969 and May 10, 1973.* Pasted-up by John Lofland and Dennis Dingemans as a Working Document for the Larkey Project of the Publications Committee of the Davis Historical Society. Copy archived at the Hattie Weber Museum of Davis.
9. Larkey, Joann Leach and Shipley Walters. 1987. *Yolo County: Land of Changing Patterns, An Illustrated History.* Northridge, CA: Windsor Publications, Inc.
10. Livingston and Blayney City and Regional Planners. 1961. *Davis Core Area Plan.* San Francisco, CA: Livingston and Blayney.
11. Lofland, John. 1999. *Old North Davis: Guide to Walking a Traditional Neighborhood.* Woodland, CA: Yolo County Historical Society.
12. ———. 2000. *Davis Heritage Buildings, How Many to Start With, How Many Left?* Yolo County Historical Booklet Series, Number 7. Woodland, CA: Yolo County Historical Society.
13. ———. 2001. *Davis City Council Elections, 1917–2000.* Yolo County Historical Booklet Series, Number 8. Woodland, CA: Yolo County Historical Society.
14. ———. 2003. *Demolishing a Historic Hotel: A Sociology of Preservation Failures in Davis, California.* Davis, CA: Davis Research.

References

15. Lofland, John and Phyllis Haig. 2000. *Davis, California, 1910–1940s*. Charleston, SC: Arcadia Publishing.

16. Lofland, John and Lyn H. Lofland. 1987. "Lime Politics: The Selectively Progressive Ethos of Davis, California." *Research in Political Sociology*. 3: 245–268.

17. McKenney, L.M. 1880. *McKenney's District Directory of 1879–80 of Sacramento . . . and Yolo Counties, Including all Residents, with Sketch of Cities and Towns . . .* Sacramento and San Francisco, CA: L.M. McKenney Publisher.

18. Menand, Louis. 2001. "College: The End of the Golden Age," *The New York Review of Books*, October 18, pp. 44–47.

19. Patten, Marjorie. 1923."The Church at the Center—Davis, California," Pp. 123–134 in Edmund Brunner, ed., *Churches of Distinction in Town and Country*. New York, NY: George Doran.

20. Pierce, George Washington, Elder and Younger, 1888–1928. *Daily Journal*. Department of Special Collections, University Library, University of California, Davis. Transcribed by Richard N. Schwab.

21. Presbyterian Church of Davisville, California. 1997. *Minutes of the Session and Register of Communicants, 13 November 1873–14 April 1918*. Transcribed by Clare L. Childers. Woodland, CA: Yolo County Historical Society.

22. Riley, Elizabeth. 1948. *The History of the California Almond Industry, 1850–1934*. Sacramento, CA: California Almond Growers Exchange [typescript in the Archives of the The Hattie Weber Museum of Davis].

23. Rothstein, Morton. 1987. *The California Wheat Kings*. Davis: Library Associates of the University Library, Davis. Keepsake Number 11.

24. Scheuring, Ann E. 2001. *Abundant Harvest: A History of the University of California, Davis*. Davis, CA: UC Davis History Project.

25. Scott, William Henry. 1900. "Davisville: A Condensed History of the Town, its Business Enterprises and Future Prospects," *Davis Enterprise*, three part series published on January 5, 12, 19.

26. Vaught, David. 1999. *Cultivating California: Growers, Specialty Crops, and Labor, 1875–1920*. Baltimore, MD: The John Hopkins University Press.

27. ———. 2003. "After the Gold Rush: Replicating the Rural Midwest in the Sacramento Valley." *Western Historical Quarterly* 34: 447–467 (Winter).

28. Williams, Henry T. 1877. *The Pacific Tourist, An Illustrated Trans-Continental Guide*. New York, NY: Henry T. Williams.

29. Woman's Christian Temperance Union Davisville Chapter. 1997. *Minutes of the Meetings, February 1888–December 1908*. Transcribed by Clare L. Childers. Woodland, CA: The Yolo County Historical Society.

INDEX

Index